D1274272

UNSDRI

UNITED NATIONS SOCIAL DEFENCE RESEARCH INSTITUTE

THE DEATH PENALTY

a bibliographical research

Publication No. 32
Rome, July 1988

Reprinted with permission of:
Revue Internationale de Droit Pénal

58e année – nouvelle série
3e et 4e trimestres 1987

Editions Erès
19, rue Gustave-Coubert, 31400 Toulouse (France)

United Nations Social Defence Research Institute
(UNSDRI)
Via Giulia 52, 00186 Rome, Italy

United Nations Publication
Sales No. E.88.III.N.3

ISBN 92-9078-006-1

TABLE OF CONTENTS

FOREWORD

This small volume presents recent work of the United Nations Social Defence Research Institute on the question of the death penalty[1] *— a matter of long-standing concern to the Institute. The book is a product of the Institute's participation in the International Conference on the Death Penalty, convened by the International Institute of Higher Studies in Criminal Sciences, in Siracusa, Italy, from 17 to 22 May 1987. The contents are part of the Acts of the Conference published by the Revue Internationale de Droit Pénal. We are grateful to the publishers of the Review for making the publication of this reprint possible.*

The International Institute of Higher Studies in Criminal Sciences organized the International Conference with the co-sponsorship of the International Association of Penal Law, the International Society for Criminology, the International Society for Social Defence and the International Penal and Penitentiary Foundation.

Apart from UNSDRI, two other units of the United Nations co-operated with the International Institute in the holding of the Conference: the UN Centre for Human Rights, and the Crime Prevention and Criminal Justice Branch of the UN Centre for Social Development and Humanitarian Affairs.

The Conference was the first major international gathering dedicated to the death penalty question for over a decade. Organizationally speaking, it emanated from a relationship of well established collaboration between United Nations bodies and major non-governmental organizations in the crime prevention and criminal justice field. One hundred and twentyfive participants from 39 countries and international organizations got together for a rich and stimulating exchange of ideas, experiences, aspirations and hopes centred on a belief in the value of human life. Looking retrospectively and at the future, participants focussed on many legal, social, political and psycho-

logical issues related to capital punishment. While complete unanimity on this question was not achieved, the discussion led to a consensus on the necessity of restricting the prescription, use and application of the death penalty and, in case of retention of the measure, its submission to safeguards arising from concern for human and legal rights.

A panel on United Nations Research and Activities on the death penalty question was organized by UNSDRI within the framework of the Conference. Presentations were made not only by UNSDRI representatives, but also by Professor Dušan Cotič, member, UN Committee on Crime Prevention and Control, and Professor Marc J. Bossuyt, Special Rapporteur of the UN Sub-Commission on the Prevention of Discrimination and the Protection of Minorities. Professor Bossuyt's presentation covered, inter-alia, *the draft Second Optional Protocol to the International Covenant on Civil and Political Rights aimed at abolition of the death penalty.*

I take this opportunity to acknowledge the contributions of our librarian, Ms. Maria Elena Andreotti and her predecessor Ms. Maria Parmeggiani, to the International Bibliography on Capital Punishment. Thanks for this bibliography must also go to Ms. Margaret Nicora. We hope to update the bibliography on a periodic basis in the future.

Rome, June 1988

Ugo Leone
Director

UNSDRI'S ACTIVITIES RELATED TO THE DEATH PENALTY ISSUES

U. LEONE*

Within the framework of the United Nations the question of capital punishment is closely linked to the human rights issue. The history of the United Nations concern with the death penalty in the field of crime control and criminal justice system dates back to 1949 when the International penal and penitentiary commission decided to undertake a coordinated effort to study the question of the death penalty. A more systematic effort to study this question was initiated in 1959 by resolution 1396 (XIV) of the General Assembly. Subsequently two substantive reports were prepared. The first report entitled « Capital Punishment » was prepared by Professor Marc Ancel in 1962. It dealt with legal theory, problems of practical application, sociological and criminological aspects of the issue, deterrent effects of capital punishment and public opinion and specialists' position regarding the death penalty. In 1967 the second report (Capital Punishment : Developments, 1961-1965) was prepared by Professor Norval Morris, which was also based upon replies to questionnaires sent out to member states and specialists, and which also dealt with controversies, the practice of capital punishment and alternatives. The issuance of these two reports led to a number of resolutions and reports all of which, to some extent, expressed a gradual shift of the United Nations position from that of the concerned but neutral observer to that of support for the eventual abolition of the death penalty. This position was expressed in the General Assembly Resolution 32/61 and Economic and Social Council resolutions 1574 (L), 1745 (LIV) and 1930 (LVIII) :

(*)Director UNSDRI.

The abovementioned resolutions also called for periodic information from Member States as well as the persuance of scientific studies on capital punishment within social, cultural, legal, political and economic contexts. In 1973 a report of the Secretary General on capital punishment was prepared based on answers received from States following which ECOSOC in resolution 1745 (LIV) requested that the reports on capital punishment be updated over five-year intervals. At the Sixth United Nations Congress on the Prevention of Crime and the Treatment of Offenders (Caracas, 25 August-5 September, 1980) the question of capital punishment was considered at length. The Crime Prevention and Criminal Justice Branch prepared a questionnaire report on capital punishment which discussed practices, the legal status and other related aspects of the issue. However, the Sixth Congress took no action on a number of proposals regarding the death penalty. In 1984 ECOSOC in its resolution 1984/50 approved the safeguards guaranteeing protection of the rights of those facing the death penalty. The seventh United Nations Congress (Milan, 25 August-6 September, 1985) considered the abovementioned safeguards and in its Resolution 15 endorsed the safeguards inviting all Member States retaining the death penalty to adopt and implement them. Discussions during the Seventh Congress were also based on the Secretary General Report entitled Social Development Questions : Capital Punishment which was prepared for ECOSOC in April 1985. This report followed similar methodology to that of previous reports.

Further incentives to studies on capital punishment came from the ECOSOC Resolution adopted in 1986 upon recommendation of the Committee on Crime Prevention and Control which, *inter alia,* requests a report on the implementation of the safeguards and a study on the question of the death penalty and new contributions of the crime-related sciences on this matter. The Crime Prevention and Criminal Justice Branch has recently published a special issue of its Newsletter devoted to capital punishment.

UNSDRI, as the interregional institute, has shown constant interest in reviewing research on capital punishment. Expressions of this interest are the International Bibliography on Capital Punishment and the report « Main Trends in Research on Capital Punishment, 1979-1986 » ; both of which have been distributed to the participants in this Conference.

The International Bibliography on Capital Punishment is the expression of the need to promote comprehensive understanding of this complex issue. It is the result of a long-standing compilation which UNSDRI initiated in 1971. Previous editions of the bibliography were compiled in 1977 and 1984 ; the present one covers approximately a fifty-year period, up to March 1987. Its compilation was based on the resources of the Institute's library and on the scanning of major abstracts, periodicals and indexes of prominent libraries, research institutes and international articles from scholarly journals, reviews of books, yearbooks and United Nations and Council of Europe documents and publications. Penal codes, encyclopaedias, university dissertations, articles from newspapers and popular magazines, audiovisual materials, unpublished papers and works of fiction have been excluded. The paucity of bibliographic references and problems concerning the availability of some publications from some regions, may have resulted in the unwitting omission of some titles. Therefore, it would be much appreciated if any of the participants to this Conference could provide us with relevant references, since it is our intention to continue with periodical up-dating of this bibliography.

The report on Research on Capital Punishment is an up-dated version of the report initially prepared for the already cited 1985 Secretary General's Report on Capital Punishment. UNSDRI'S report covers the period from 1979 to 1986, discusses the volume of research carried out and analyses the main characteristics of specific topics regarding the capital punishment issue.

MAIN TRENDS IN RESEARCH ON CAPITAL PUNISHMENT (1979-1986*)

U. ZVEKIC** et T. KUBO***

I. Introduction

This report[1] provides basic information on the characteristics of research on capital punishment published from January 1979 to December 1986. In particular, the purpose is to present a quantitative and qualitative analysis of major trends in the period under review. Although the period covered is not long enough to arrive at definite conclusions concerning general trends, the data analyzed here provides a basis for drawing certain tentative conclusions.

This survey is based on materials available in the UNSDRI library and thus it reflects the possible non-representativeness of the library collection ; in other words, the possible bias of the data itself might, to some extent, distort the deriving of generalizations. Also this survey covers only works that have been published and

(*) This is a revised version of the following article : Zvekic, U., F. Saito & N. Ghirlando : « Main trends in research on capital punishment, 1979-1983 ». *Crime Prevention and Criminal Justice Newsletter,* no. 12/13, pp. 54-61, November 1986.

(**) Research Officer, UNSDRI.

(***) Associate Research Officer, UNSDRI.

(1) As a supplement to this report, an International Bibliography on Capital Punishment (UNSDRI, Rome, March 1987) have been compiled. S. *infra,* Part. VIII.

does not cover current research studies which have not yet been published. The aim is not to summarize research results but rather to present a general description of the characteristics of research activity which prevail in the field of capital-punishment.

Finally, it should be noted that the research studies analyzed below deal only with the legally-defined death penalty. Extra-legal or extra-judicial executions are excluded from the analysis.

II. A quantitative survey of research on capital punishment

As mentioned in the introduction, the period under consideration was not long enough to allow for an analysis of the general trends over time in terms of the volume of research or adequate coverage of major topics. Thus, what follows refers only to the description of the characteristics of what was presumed to be a significant share of research on capital punishment, covering, as much as possible, volume, origin, scope, methods applied, basic premises and subject matter. It should be noted that the basic classification scheme was built up in relation to the subject matter of the research, the definitions of which will be given later.

Subject matter by year

The number of published works categorized by subject matter and by year is shown in Table 1, which is the basis of this review. There are a total of 363 published works, an average of 45.4 per year. The number of publications that have been identified either in reference form, abstract form or document form in the covered period is 562[2]. This means that, on average, about 65 percent of the identified published works are reviewed in this report. The percentage of reviewed works per year varies from 45 percent in 1985 to 77 percent in 1979 and in 1981. 199 works which have not been reviewed are mainly published in various law journals in the United States.

The classification categories are the same as those in the previous UNSDRI report[3], where six categories were extracted from

(2) See the Appendix of this report for a detailed quantitative analysis of the published works that have been identified.

(3) Initially the UNSDRI report was prepared for the Report of the Secretary-General : Social Development Question – Capital Punishment, Doc. E/1985/43, 26 April 1985. Later published as : Zvekic, U., F. Saito & N. Ghirlando « Main trends in research on capital punishment, 1979-1983 ». *Crime Prevention and Criminal Justice Newsletter,* no. 12/13, Pp. 54-61, November 1986.

TABLE 1
NUMBER OF PUBLICATIONS BY SUBJECT
Subject Matter

Year	General Debate	Legal Issues	Application of Capital Punishment	Attitudes towards Capital Punishment	Measurement of Deterrent Effects	Death Row Inmates	Total
1979	15	16	6	5	12	4	58
1980	7	16	5	4	9	3	44
1981	9	16	7	3	5	4	44
1982	17	18	4	4	10	1	54
1983	19	16	5	4	9	1	54
1984	12	19	12	8	2	0	53
1985	10	9	6	3	1	0	29
1986	8	9	5	2	0	3	27
Total	97	119	50	33	48	16	363

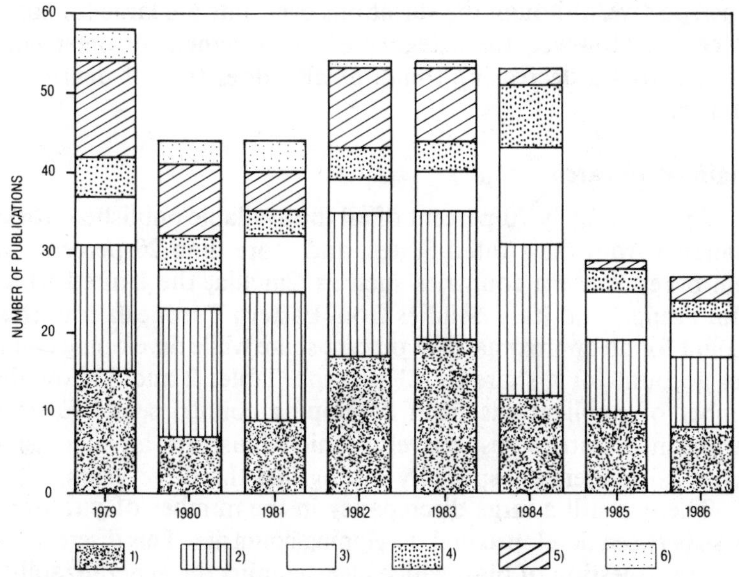

the 254 works. These six categories are 1) general debate ; 2) legal issues ; 3) application of capital punishment ; 4) attitudes towards capital punishment ; 5) measurement of deterrence effects and 6) death row inmates.

As shown in Table 1, there are notable differences in the number of published works by subject matter. Materials on legal issues consist of 119 works (32.9 percent of the total), followed by studies classified as general debate (26.5 percent) and research in the area of deterrence effects (13.3 percent). Application of capital punishment and attitudes towards it comprise 13.8 percent and 9.1 percent respectively. The topic of death row inmates is the one least dealt with among them (4.4 percent). Comparing the results with those of the previous study, the areas of general debate and legal issues remain almost the same (26.4 percent and 26.5 percent for the former category and 32.3 percent and 32.9 percent for the latter). The areas of application of capital punishment and of attitudes towards it increase from 10.6 percent to 13.8 percent for the former and from 7.9 percent to 9.1 percent for the latter.

On the other hand, the topics of measurement of deterrence effects and of death row inmates were dealt with less frequently (from 17.7 percent to 13.3 percent for the former and from 5.1 percent to 4.4 percent for the latter). As regards the subject matters themselves, general trends in the number of publications are relatively stable in the categories of general debate, of legal issues and of perspective, although the variations over time are large for some categories. However, the category of measurement of deterrence effects shows a decreasing trend, as also does that of death row inmates.

Origin of research

Approximately 70 percent of all the available published works emanated from the United States, and more than 20 percent are from other Western countries such as Canada, the United Kingdom, France, and Italy. Studies from Eastern European countries account for an approximately 1 percent share while developing countries account for a share of 4.1 percent. Tables 2 and 3 show the number of publications from developing countries and Eastern European countries respectively, which illustrate an increasing numerical tendency, especially during last the three years.

There is still a large discrepancy in the number of published works between developed and developing countries. This discrepancy raises the question of bias, which clearly limits the generalizability of the results of the analysis. This bias may be due to shortcomings in the UNSDRI library collection, but it may also reflect, at least to some extent, the « really biased » state of research on capital punishment : in other words, there is less research on capital punishment in developing countries in correspondence with the general state of research in them. It may also reflect the different situations of abolitionist movements or sentiments in various countries, as well as political, legislative and judicial responses to them. It

TABLE 2
NUMBER OF PUBLICATIONS BY SUBJECT
CONCERNING DEVELOPING COUNTRIES
Subject Matter

Year	General Debate	Legal Issues	Application of Capital Punishment	Attitudes towards Capital Punishment	Measurement of Deterrent Effects	Death Row Inmates	Total
1979	0	0	0	0	0	0	0
1980	0	0	0	0	0	0	0
1981	0	0	0	0	0	0	0
1982	1	0	1	0	0	0	2
1983	0	0	0	0	1	0	1
1984	3	1	2	0	0	0	6
1985	1	0	0	0	0	0	1
1986	3	0	1	1	0	0	5
Total	8	1	4	1	1	0	15

TABLE 3
NUMBER OF PUBLICATIONS BY SUBJECT
CONCERNING EASTERN EUROPEAN COUNTRIES
Subject Matter

Year	General Debate	Legal Issues	Application of Capital Punishment	Attitudes towards Capital Punishment	Measurement of Deterrent Effects	Death Row Inmates	Total
1979	0	0	0	0	0	0	0
1980	0	0	0	0	0	0	0
1981	0	0	0	0	0	0	0
1982	0	0	0	0	0	0	0
1983	0	0	0	0	0	0	0
1984	1	0	0	0	0	0	1
1985	0	0	1	0	0	0	1
1986	1	0	0	0	0	0	1
Total	2	0	1	0	0	0	3

may also be reflective of differences in the state of legal problems involved in the application of capital punishment. Finally, some topics such as measurement of deterrence effects, based on « before-after » comparisons are in fact limited to countries or regions which have experienced *de jure* or *de facto* changes in the status of capital punishment.

It should be noted that a major part of the research from the United States related to the legal provisions on the death penalty reviewed by the United States Supreme Court.

Scope of research

Approximately 85 percent of the published works represent a mono-cultural type of research dealing with problems specific to one country or one culture. About 15 percent belong to a cross-cultural type of research in very broad terms ; most of them make simple comparisons of situations in different countries. However, it can also be said that works categorized as general debate have, by their nature, some universal or cross-cultural connotations, references and importance even though they refer to one country.

It should be pointed out that more cross-cultural type of research is needed for understanding the nature of capital punishment within the framework of integrated legal, social and political structures.

Methods applied in research

There are three major groups in terms of methods used in the research : legal-normative approaches, behavioural science approaches and the combination of these two types. There is clear association between the subject matter and the methods applied. The majority of works in the category of legal issues are characterized by the use of legal-normative approaches ; while studies in the categories of measurement of deterrence effects and of application of death penalty are predominantly utilizing behavioural science approaches. However, it should be noted that about one third of the published works utilize a combination of these two approaches, which tends to spread to the area where traditionally one or the other method was exclusively applied. Such interdisciplinary approaches where various types of methods are utilized to multidimensionally analyse the phenomenon may facilitate the better understanding of a complex phenomenon such as capital punishment.

Basic premise

This concerns the ideological position on the « pro » or « con » of capital punishment. It can be stated that the neutral position is reflected in the majority of research studies in the period under consideration.

However, there is some association between the subject matter and the basic premise. Research on the measurement of deterrence effects and materials on the legal issues tend to be neutral in terms of basic premises, while in the area of general debate these tend to have a more explicit position. It is also noted that, when a position is expressed, it refers more often the abolitionist's position rather than that of the retentionist's.

III. **Review of the major topics**

The following discussion aims at providing, for the period under consideration, not a summary of all the research findings but rather some insights into thematic and methodological concerns and principal findings.

General debate

The issue of capital punishment is of great relevance and has been the subject of debate in the past, as it is in the present, and as it will be in the future. It involves ethical, religious and political components which are highly interwoven. Its peculiar nature, interrelated with fundamental values of contemporary society, the recent trend towards its re-introduction in the legal systems of a number of countries, as well as the dissimilarities between public opinion, scientists' approaches, and political and legal responses to the question are some of the explanations for the topical importance of capital punishment.

Since ancient times one powerful stream of thought considered the death penalty as a means for the protection of the fundamental values of the community. As legal systems became organized and the rule of law developed, legislative provisions were formulated to fulfill the aims of retribution and, later on, deterrence. These two basic principles, retained in the criminal laws of our times, constitute the perennial issues on which scientits, politicians, philosophers, lawyers and the general public continue to focus using different approaches and rationales.

The debate for and against capital punishment, was set out at the end of the 18th century and still goes on unresolved and perhaps unresolvable. Although the debate centers around typical arguments used by both sides, its frequency, the form it takes and the particular arguments underlined in the debate are, to a large extent, influenced by the particular cases which may arouse public sentiments which, in turn, shape the debate.

Apart from the situational factors, the debate is supported by two contrasting trends. On the one hand, there is a trend towards its abolition or restricted use, as exemplified by *de jure* and *de facto* changes introduced in an increasing number of countries, namely, Western European and Latin American countries. In particular, these changes entail the *de jure* or *de facto* suppression of the death penalty, the decrease in the number of offences punishable by death and the suspension *sine die* of its execution. On the other hand, the opposite trend also appears, as exemplified by the retention, re-introduction and use of death penalty in a number of countries. Both these trends are interrelated with prevailing political and social conditions.

The contemporary debate on the death penalty is complex and characterized by divergent and often incompatible views and has often been compared to a dialogue among the deaf. Conceptual assumptions of proponents and opponents on the issue are quite different and analyses based on these different assumptions inevitably lead to opposite conclusions. Two major aspects of the death penalty question still dominate the debate : the retributive aspect, where the function of the death penalty is considered to be primarily for satisfying society's demand for vengeance, and the preventive aspect, where the function is primarily deterrence. Both the retentionists and the abolitionists focus their arguments on these two aspects, drawing on the moral and scientific evidence which best upholds their views. Furthermore, both take into consideration the ethical and the utilitarian components of capital punishment. However, those emphasizing the retributive aspect argue more from the ethical perspective, while those concerned with the deterrence principle give more weight to the utilitarian aspect. The contrast between ethics and politics still permeates the debate over the rationale and justification of the death penalty.

Legal issues

Analysis of the present legal research shows the state of « legal mind » and legal affairs. The legal and moral debate concerning the constitutionality of the death penalty, which dominated the field for a long time, has slowed down. There seems to be a shift from the issue of constitutionality to the concern with procedural safeguards involved in the process of imposing capital punishment. Emphasis, which used to be on the problem of « pro » or « con » of capital punishment, is now on procedural guarantees to reduce the risk of arbitrariness in legal procedure. In this sense, there is a shift from moral to technical arguments. Legal research, in the strict sense, is dominantly instrumental, following legislative or court practice, although the concern with procedure has a value of its own.

There are at least four topics largely discussed in legal research. They are 1) the appellate review, 2) the « death qualified » jury, 3) the issue of evidence, including psychiatric testimony, and 4) the application of capital punishment for minors. The first and the third topics are closely related to procedural safeguards, while the second topic is related to the problem of arbitrariness. Recently, many arguments have been concerned with the areas of death qualification of the jury and of the application of the death penalty to minors.

It is noticed that legal analysis tends to become more and more combined with social science analysis where a social phenomenon is analyzed on the basis of empirical data on factors affecting the process of case handling. There are, of course, many studies which utilize traditional combinations of legal, philosophical and historical analyses. While legal-social science analysis is more neutral in terms of the abolitionist-retentionist question, legal-philosophical analysis takes a much clearer position, whether pro-abolitionist or pro-retentionist.

There are some, but not many, studies which discuss the adequacy of the death penalty for new types of crimes from the viewpoints of legal and crime control perspectives.

As regards the problem of arbitrariness in legal decision-making processes, it is generally recognized that arbitrariness should be minimized. Research on judicial practice indicates, however, that there exists inconsistencies due to either different interpretations of legal norms or to variations of social-political value systems among those involved in the cases. It would seem that personal preferences and different value judgements are unavoidable in legal reasoning, regardless of the extent to which the legal system attempts to be impersonal. Because of this factor, it is entirely appropriate to have, within the given legal system, strict procedural safeguards in order to reduce arbitrariness and to protect human rights as well as to accomplish « justice ».

Analysis of court practice shows that in many instances the court tends to address issues for which guidelines already exist, leaving « trouble aspects » untouched. This tendency is present not only in the topic of capital punishment but in legal decision-making in general because of the formality-outcome approach in legal reasoning. Nevertheless, concern with the procedural safeguards for reducing arbitrariness is of paramount importance because of the unique consequence of capital punishment.

Legal research which has pointed out the existence of arbitrariness, although concerned with technical matters, has presented support for the argument of abolition of capital punishment.

Application of death penalty

This category covers issues such as trends in the current use of capital punishment at national, regional and international levels. It includes differential treatment of crimes as well as of defendants, which appears to be the major issue in the field.

More than half of the reported works deal with the issue of « discrimination in the criminal justice system », and most of the studies in this subcategory come from the United States. The major concern of these studies is racial discrimination in the criminal justice system, especially in the imposition of capital punishment. Based on statistical analysis of the data, some works argue that capital punishment has been, both in the past and even in the present, imposed disproportionately to non-white defendants. Other studies argue that the race of the victim, not the race of the defendant, has significant influence on the imposition of capital punishment. Still others suggest that the determinant factor in the process of imposing capital punishment is not race but the socio-economic status of the defendant. It is also stated that the sex of both victim and defendant has some influence. Geographical differences in sentencing of the death penalty have also been recognized. Thus, most of the studies have concluded that, to some extent, discrimination exists in the criminal justice system.

Other works in this category are of a descriptive type, presenting the results of surveys on the imposition of capital punishment and on actual execution. Because of the lack of reliable statistics concerning capital punishment, in some regions, it is difficult to trace the global trends in actual execution of the death penalty. It should be emphasized that more research effort is needed on the general trends of the application of capital punishment as well as on the collection of reliable statistics at the global level.

Attitude towards death penalty

Public attitudes and sentiments toward capital punishment are the major topic in this category. The issues discussed can be classified into three main groups. The first group focuses on public attitudes regarding capital punishment within the scope of punishment in general. The second group focuses on the relationship between public attitudes and legislative, judicial and/or political situations. The third focuses on the beliefs or reasoning processes underlying these attitudes. All these issues are highly interrelated. Most studies deal with public support for either abolition or retention of capital punishment. Some studies are closely related to the topics of legal issues and of application of capital punishment because they examine the effects of the attitude of juries on their decision-making processes.

Public attitudes toward capital punishment are given much attention by researchers because the findings could be used to support « pro » or « con » position. However, the problem has turned out to be not that simple. Various studies indicate that attitudes can be determined by the various combinations of several factors and that even the same attitude can be the product of different underlying factors. Another point indicated is that the nature of attitudes is not yet well known. There are discussions about the possibility of attitude changes in various ways. On the other hand, other arguments insist that if attitudes can be changed relatively easily, then they are not determinants of behaviour. Studies suggest that the attitude toward a social phenomenon is one thing and the actual behaviour concerning it (e.g. political behaviour, such as voting) quite another. The appropriateness of public attitude as an adequate basis for legislation is also examined.

Research has pointed out that the nature of public knowledge about caital punishment remains unknown to a large extent or at least that it has only been partially examined. It is suggested that mere counting of attitudes toward capital punishment may be misleading or unreliable for legal or political action or both, because of the unknown nature of the relation between knowledge and social action. It is also noted that public attitudes fluctuate widely, especially toward serious crimes eliciting strong emotional reactions.

Recent research is generally oriented toward examining the nature of public knowledge and social and psychological processes underlying attitudes toward capital punishment. Understanding the process of attitude formation and the effect of attitudes on actual behaviour, as well as the basic belief and logic underlying the attitude, can illuminate the discrepancy between public attitudes and the abolitionist norm, even in countries where capital punishment has been abolished for several decades.

In contrast to earlier research where public opinion toward capital punishment was examined, recent studies tend to differenciate between magnitudes of attitude, on the one hand, and social and psychological factors underlying attitudes, on the other. Empirical studies have found that, although the overt attitude may be either « pro » or « con » with regard to the capital penalty, there exist several clusters of factors underlying the attitude, such as utilitarian, humanitarian, instrumental, ethical, etc. Also, attitudes toward capital punishment are related to attitudes on crime, the criminal justice system and other social phenomena. These relationships are not always straightforward.

Similarly, research has questioned earlier findings explaining support for capital punishment as being based on belief in its deterrent effects as commonly indicated in public polls. Although such belief can be one reason for supporting capital punishment, it is not necessarily the only one. Recent studies indicate that there are various underlying factors that can be treated as the basis for social and political value systems. Therefore, although the relation between support of capital punishment end belief in deterrence seems to be the motive, or the major sustaining factor, for the pro-death penalty position, such belief appears to be a cognitive justification, often unconscious, for a more fundamental value system which actually determines social and political behaviour.

It is interesting to note that, although they express strong beliefs, both abolitionists and retentionists show little knowledge about the administration of capital punishment. This discrepancy questions the appropriateness of public attitude as the sole basis for legislative change.

An attitude towards capital punishment is not simply a response to concerns or experience related to crime, but rather a facet of a general social-political ideology and value system. Opinion polls, the results of which have often been used to support either « pro » or « con » positions on capital punishment and which were usually based on a small number of questions about the death penalty, sometimes obscured the complexity of this phenomenon. Recent research has suggested that the issue cannot be examined adequately through the analysis of simple opinion polls from the public or from experts.

Research on public attitudes toward capital punishment should be examined within the theoretical framework of attitude in general, as a social, psychological and political phenomenon.

Measurement of deterrent effects

Deterrent effects are a central issue of the capital punishment debate. Studies in this category have tried to examine whether the various aspects of the death penalty actually have deterrent effects.

More than half of the studies are empirical. Four types of approaches are dominantly employed to measure the deterrent effects of capital punishment :

1 – longitudinal or time-series studies, where the co-variation between the murder rate and the execution of the death penalty are examined ;

2 – comparison of the crime rate, especially homicide rate, « before » and « after » the abolition or reinstallation of capital punishment within the same region, wherein the change of homicide rate is analyzed and explained in terms of the change of legislation ;

3 – short-term effects of execution, wherein the change in the number of reported murders shortly after the publicized execution of the death penalty is examined ;

4 – cross-sectional comparison, in which murder rates between abolitionist and retentionist countries or regions are examined.

Nearly three-quarters of the empirical studies have reported no significant relation between capital punishment and the murder rate. Some of the studies indicate that the execution of death penalty and the murder rate are independent phenomena and that socio-economic and demographic factors can be better predictors of the murder rate than the number of executions of the death penalty. Some cross-sectional studies report that abolition of capital punishment is often followed by a decrease in the murder rate. On the other hand, several studies also claim that capital punishment does, to some extent, have a detterent effect or at least a short-term impact on the murder rate.

Most studies use the murder rate as an indicator in measuring possible deterrence effects and little attention is paid to exploring other appropriate indicators.

Because the studies in this category require empirical findings to verify the existence or non-existence of deterrent effects, methodological problems involved in measuring deterrent effects also attract researchers' attention. Some of the major issues in methodology can be summarized as follows :

a) even if co-variations between capital punishment and the murder rate are found, they do not necessarily indicate a causal relation between them. There always is the possibility that other uncontrolled factors are influencing both. When comparative methods are used, the variation of the murder rate need not necessarily be attributed to the capital punishment factor. When sophisticated methods of quantitative analysis are applied and when it is concluded that the variations in the murder rate are statistically explained by the capital punishment factor, it does not necessarily mean that models underlying the analysis are correct.

b) sometimes adequate data are not available for the analysis ; also insufficient or inadequate data in terms of quality and quantity are used for analysis.

c) as mentioned above, indicators used for measuring deterrence are not always carefully examined in terms of their appropriateness for the purpose ;

d) for this subject matter adequately controlled experiments are impossible. Inferential procedures have to be used based on observation of a situation which happens to have only some similarity with the quasi-experimental setting ;

e) the basic assumption of the deterrence hypothesis is that potential criminals are rational and they calculate costs-benefits before they actually commit crimes. However, such an assumption is itself questionable, especially when the murder rate is used as an indicator of deterrence, because it is recognized that emotional conditions play a significant role in a large number of murder cases.

The findings of the reported studies do not settle the debate over the deterrent effect of capital punishment, although the general trend supports the non-existence of the effect. This debate is still open both in terms of theoretical argument and methodological considerations. The results based on statistical data as well as their application that go beyond their intrinsic values and limitations hould be used with caution.

Death row inmates

The major issue in this topic is the examination and classification of psychological, sociological and criminological characteristics of death row inmates. All of these studies were carried out in the United States where public access to death row inmates is relatively open. There are several studies which gather information from criminal records, observation within the institution and personal interviews with death row inmates. Some of them found that the majority of death row inmates were first-time offenders with no prior criminal record of violence, and that about five percent of the inmates believed they had received unfair trials. Also indicated is the fact that psychological characteristics such as apathy, powerlessness and mental disturbance are often found among death row inmates. In relation to findings that a considerable number of inmates suffer from mental disturbances, the present legal procedures for assessing the state of sanity are also examined, and it is suggested that more comprehensive procedures for the protection of human rights is necessary. In addition, accessability of public and press to the execution of death penalties, as well as the inmates rights, draw the attention of researchers.

IV. Conclusion

Most of the research reported comes from the United States and Western developed countries. More research is needed from other parts of the world, especially from the developing countries, although the number of publications from the latter has been increasing recently. An expanded research effort in developing countries, together with more research in developed countries, should permit greater cross-cultural and situational comparisons and facilitate an understanding of questions emerging from specific social, cultural and legal-political milieux within the framework of a global context.

This survey of thematic and methodological concerns and characteristics of capital punishment research for the period between 1979 and 1986 shows that there has been no major break-through in terms of the issues dealt with. The debate for and against capital punishment continues, following paths laid down a long time ago.

In developed countries, the spectrum of research issues on capital punishment spans a wide range of concerns. On the other hand, in developing countries, it seems that most research is restricted to the areas of general debate and of the application of the death penalty.

The subject matter is now permeated more than ever before by empirical verifications coming from legal and social science analyses, at least in the developed countries. Although this verification is inconclusive in terms of upholding any one position, it improves the state of art in terms of understanding the complex nature of the issue.

Appendix

In the report, only the materials available in the UNSDRI library were analyzed. However, as a supplement to the report, an International Bibliography on Capital Punishment was compiled covering all the studies that have been identified in the form of reference materials, abstracts or documentation. The analysis of these materials may suggest some trends in the research on capital punishment.

The number of publications that have been identified is shown in Table A-1.

In the 1950s there were 123 publications, an average of 12.3 per year. In the 1960s, 334 studies have been counted, an average of 33.4 per year. In the 1970s, the number of published works rapidly increased to 625, an average of 62.5 per year, nearly twice as large as that of the previous decade. This increase might reflect people's concern about capital punishment and the wide spread of the abolitionist movement. It might also be influenced by the pending decision of the U.S. Supreme Court on the constitutionality of capital

TABLE A-1
NUMBER OF PUBLICATIONS

Year	Publications	Year	Publications	Year	Publications
Before 1939	73	1950	5	1970	42
		1951	4	1971	48
		1952	19	1972	62
1940-49	18	1953	12	1973	64
		1954	9	1974	81
		1955	11	1975	54
		1956	16	1976	50
		1957	17	1977	71
		1958	11	1978	79
		1959	19	1979	75
		1960	24	1980	61
		1961	37	1981	57
		1962	30	1982	72
		1963	20	1983	91
		1964	54	1984	90
		1965	20	1985	65
		1966	29	1986	51
		1967	26		
		1968	24		
no date	5	1969	70		
				Total	1 667

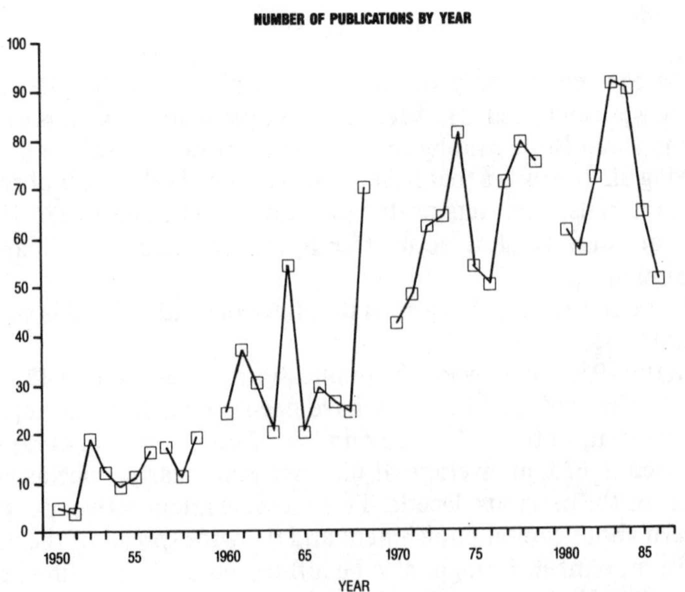

punishment, which promoted not only legal studies but also social science studies on capital punishment, including the measurement of deterrence. This tendency still continues in the 1980s even after the U.S. Supreme Court decision that the death penalty does not invariably violate the prohibition of cruel and unusual punishment as defined by the Eighth Amendment of the U.S. Constitution. By the end of 1986, 479 studies have been identified, an average of 68.4 per year. However, the characteristics of research on capital punishment have changed since then, as described in detail in this report, especially in the review of major topics.

As regards published works in developing countries, the number of publications is shown in Table A-2.

There were only 4 works that have been identified in 1950s, on average 0.4 per year. In the 1960s, 10 publications were identified, an average of 1.0 per year. However, in the 1970s, the identified works increased to 27, on average 2.7 per year, nearly three times as large as that in the previous decade. This increase reflects the general tendency of increase mentioned above. By the end of 1986, 22 research works were identified, on average 3.1 per year. Till

TABLE A-2
NUMBER OF PUBLICATIONS CONCERNING
DEVELOPING COUNTRIES

Year	Publications	Year	Publications	Year	Publications
Before 1939	0	1950	1	1970	5
		1951	0	1971	2
		1952	0	1972	3
1940-49	0	1953	0	1973	7
		1954	0	1974	2
		1955	1	1975	1
		1956	1	1976	2
		1957	0	1977	2
		1958	0	1978	1
		1959	1	1979	2
		1960	0	1980	2
		1961	0	1981	1
		1962	2	1982	5
		1963	3	1983	2
		1964	0	1984	6
		1965	0	1985	1
		1966	1	1986	5
		1967	2		
		1968	0		
no date	0	1969	2		
				Total	63

the end of 1960s, the number of identified publications in developing countries were around 3 percent of the total. This became about 4.3 percent in the 1970s and 4.5 percent in the 1980s. It can be said that, although the number of publications is small, it is increasing. This increase has also been recorded in the report.

The number of identified publications in Eastern European countries is shown in Table A-3.

TABLE A-3
NUMBER OF PUBLICATIONS CONCERNING
EASTERN EUROPEAN COUNTRIES

Year	Publications	Year	Publications	Year	Publications
Before 1939	1	1950	0	1970	2
		1951	0	1971	0
		1952	0	1972	0
1940-49	0	1953	0	1973	0
		1954	0	1974	0
		1955	0	1975	0
		1956	1	1976	0
		1957	1	1977	1
		1958	0	1978	3
		1959	1	1979	3
		1960	0	1980	1
		1961	0	1981	3
		1962	1	1982	7
		1963	0	1983	3
		1964	0	1984	4
		1965	0	1985	1
		1966	2	1986	6
		1967	0		
		1968	0		
no date	1	1969	0		
				Total	42

A similar tendency of recent increase to the one in developing countries can be detected. There were only 3 works both in the 1950s and in the 1960s. In the 1970s, the identified works increased to 9, and, in the 1980s, the number of identified publications became 25, which is more than twice as many as those in the previous decades. Till the end of the 1970s, 15 works were identified in Eastern European countries, which consisted of 1.3 percent of the total. As against this, during the 1980s, identified works concerning Eastern European countries came up to 25, i.e., 5.1 percent of the total. It can therefore be stated that, although the number of publications is still rather small, there has been an increase in recent years, especially after 1981. Nevertheless, it should also be noted that the

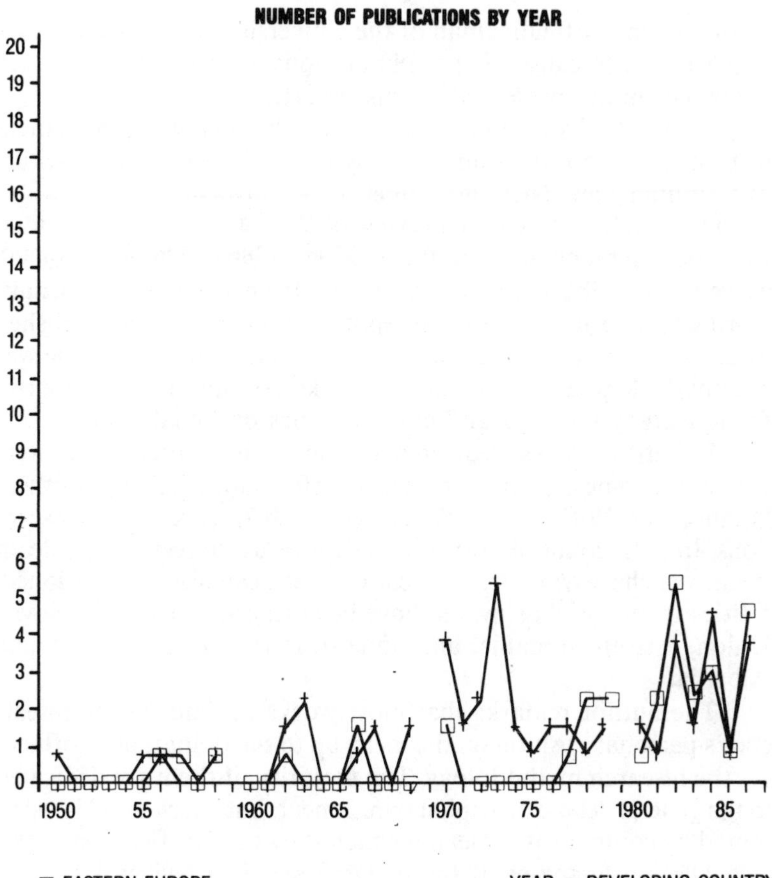

availability of these works is relatively limited. As mentioned in the report, only 3 works were available in the UNSDRI library for review. This underlies the necessity of facilitating the exchange of information among countries for wide-range cross-cultural studies on capital punishment.

For the purpose of widening the regional coverage of the report, UNSDRI sent out an enquiry to several regional experts concerning research on capital punishment and bibliographical reference materials. By the time this report was written, two replies had been received, one from Prof. Grzeskowiak of Nicholas Copernicus University in Poland (covering Eastern European countries), and the second from Prof. Glickman of the University of Botswana (covering Africa). Because of space limitations, only abstracts of each contribution are presented in this report.

Abstract of « Main trends of research on capital punishment in Eastern European countries » by Prof. Grzeskowiak, Institute of Criminal Law, Nicholas Copernicus University.

The article is based on a review of the Eastern European literature on capital punishment from 1979 to 1986 available in Poland, as well as on bibliographical references from specialized journals. During this period, no official reports on the issue were published by any one government of the countries in the area. The issue was mainly dealt with by general works like criminal law handbooks for university students and commentaries on penal codes.

Scientific works dedicated to the capital punishment were scarce, for some countries there is no information being published. Poland, with 19 titles, and Yugoslavia, with 7, represent two exceptions. In both countries, other initiatives linked to research on death penalty such as symposia, associations, etc. can also be mentioned. 5 titles from Czechoslovakia have been traced, 3 from the Soviet Union, 1 from Rumania, and none from Bulgaria, Hungary and Albania.

The author remarks that most works depend on the researcher's personal position on the issue, up to the point that it influences the research methodology. The majority of them are dedicated to the general debate on capital punishment, but a new trend is represented by comparative research which shows a significant increase.

The major topics of the research are then reviewed.

1. **General debate**

The abolitionist position can be found, together with retentionism, in Poland and in Yugoslavia. In both countries, a new approach to the problem is represented by the concern for the « right to life » supported by the International Conventions on Human Rights. In other Eastern European countries, all the works show a retentionist position, with slight differences on the question of the extent to which the application of death penalty can be legitimate.

2. **Legal issues**

In most countries, research is limited to the descriptions of existing legislations. In some Polish and Yugoslav works, the problem of reform of legislation is faced, basically from an abolitionist point of view. A few studies from Czechoslovakia and the

USSR deal with possible limitations in the application of the death penalty.

3. Application of death penalty

Very few studies on procedural issues based on the reasons for the judgement have been conducted in Poland and Yugoslavia.

4. Surveys of public attitude

A rather comprehensive survey among specialists such as judges, lawyers, psychiatrists, sociologists and university students has been conducted in Yugoslavia, showing a majority view which is in favour of retaining the death penalty but for certain types of crime only. A partial survey has been conducted in Poland, limited to the Warsaw area, within the context of a more general study on attitudes toward deviance.

5. Execution of the penalty

There is a lack of research on this topic ; the only exceptions are found in Polish and Yugoslav works which are characterized as reflecting theoretical and juridical approaches.

6. Comparative research

As already said, this represents a new trend in research. Research on the death penalty in the socialist countries has been conducted in Poland, showing the similarities of legislations among them. Research on the UN position on the death penalty has been conducted in Czechoslovakia.

The author then draws conclusions on the death penalty issue in Eastern Europe and related research.

Abstract of « Research on homicide in Botswana in relation to Main trends in research on capital punishment : 1979-1983 » by Prof. M.J.A. Glickman, Department of Sociology, University of Botswana.

The author states that there has been almost no research effort on capital punishment in the African region except Botswana. Although capital punishment has not been abolished completely in Botswana, where only treason and murder are punishable by the death penalty, the average number of executions per year is less than 1.5, and the author claims that Botswana is almost a *de facto* abolitionist country. Seven propositions are described to illustrate the legal possibility of imposing the death penalty as well as the general procedure for appeal. They are as follows : 1) An acquittal requires a cogent rebuttal of the case ; 2) When extenuating circumstances come out, a lesser sentence should be imposed ; 3) When no extenuating circumstances are revealed, the death penalty is probable ; 4) When the accused refuses to agree with the presentation of extenuating circumstances in the court because of innocent plea, the death penalty is probable ; 5) The Court of Appeal will not interfere with the trial judge's discretion unless an accused fails to attempt to rebut the case ; 6) The Court of Appeal will not interfere in the trial judge's discretion unless the trial judge is deviating from the Penal Code ; and 7) The Court of Appeal will not interfere in the trial judge's discretion unless the judge fails to take into account the extenuating circumstances. Actual cases are described briefly as examples for each of the propositions.

Although the Criminal Law in Botswana has received strong influence from both English common law and Roman-Dutch law, the concept of extenuating circumstances is somewhat different from that of mitigating factors in Great Britain, and the author describes the distinction between the two.

Concerning the debate on capital punishment in Botswana, not the length of imprisonment but the fact of imprisonment itself has a strong effect not only on offenders but also on public attitudes, which, in turn, produce stigma toward ex-prisoners.

For the purpose of reducing murder cases, the author suggests that the police check people for knife carrying, especially in drinking places. Many murders have been committed in such place by using a knife. This kind of police checking, he argues, will not violate civil liberties.

He then draws attention to the resemblance of so-called ritual murder cases in Botswana with cases in Great Britain to illustrate the potential of cross-cultural study.

Finally, the author invites attention to the desirability of further study on previous convictions of those convicted of murder charges.

While UNSDRI has not received any replies from Asia and Latin America, some information on these regions can be found in the Crime Prevention and Criminal Justice Newsletter, Special Issue on Capital Punishment [4].

---

(4) United Nations, Department of International Economic and Social Affairs, Centre for Social Development and Humanitarian Affairs (Vienna). *Crime Prevention and Criminal Justice Newsletter, Special Combined Issue on Capital Punishment,* n. 12/13, November 1986.

INTERNATIONAL BIBLIOGRAPHY ON CAPITAL PUNISHMENT

U. LEONE*

The question of the capital punishment issue is an almost perennial concern. In essence it is an ethical problem, but it is also a political, legal, sociological and psychological problem. Its complexity requires multidisciplinarity of approach. Whatever point of view and approach is taken, it should be realized that both symbolically and concretely, the problem is located in the core of relationship between the citizen and the state, furthermore, from both the national and the international perspectives it is closely related to the human rights issue. All these concerns have been reflected and continue to be embodied in the long-lasting interest and activity of the United Nations aimed at progressively reducing the use of capital punishment or the threat thereof, as well as at promoting safeguards for those condemned to death.

This International Bibliography on Capital Punishment is an expression of this concern of the United Nations. It also addresses the need to promote comprehensive understanding of this complex issue. It is the result of a long-standing compilation which the United Nations Social Defence Research Institute initiated in 1971. Its aim is to provide the international community with an extensive picture of the world literature on this topic. Previous editions of the bibliography were published in 1971 and in 1977, while an up-dated supplement was brought out in 1984. Each time many references to past literature as well as newly-published titles were added, reflecting a constant endeavour to take account of all noteworthy scientific publications related to capital punishment.

If the reader finds differences in the quantitative coverage given to various countries, this reflects differences in the degree of interest national scholars take in the topic. The paucity of bibliographic references and problems concerning the availability of some publications from some regions, may also have resulted in the unwitting omission of some titles.

The compilation of this bibliography was based on the resources of the Institute's library and on the scanning of major abstracts, periodicals and indexes of prominent libraries, research institutes and international organizations, as well as on specialized bibliographies such as that by

(*) Director U.N.S.R.I, March, 1987.

M. Vandiver and M.L. Radelet. The titles selected include monographs, articles from scholarly journals, reviews of books, yearbooks and United Nations and Council of Europe documents and publications. Penal codes, encyclopeadias, university dissertations, articles from newspapers and popular magazines, audiovisual materials, unpublished papers and works of fiction have been excluded.

UNSDRI would like to thank Professor Hugo A. Bedau, from Tufts University, U.S.A., Professor M.J.A. Glickmann, from the University of Botswana, and Professor Alicja Grześkowiak, from Nicholas Copernicus University, Poland for their help in providing additional references for this bibliography.

The bibliography has been prepared in accordance with the rules on editorial style and publication policies, procedures and practice set forth in the « United Nations Editorial Manual », New York, N.Y., 1983.

Abolition moves. Penal Reformer. London, 5, April 1939.

Abramowitz, E. and D. Paget. *Executive clemency in capital cases.* New York Law Review. New York, N.Y., 39 : 136-180. 1964.

Aćmovic, M. *Savremene dileme o smrtnoj kazni (The contemporary dilemma about capital punishment).* Pravni Zivot. Beograd. no. 4 : 437-449.

Acker, J.R. *Mandatory capital punishment fot the life term inmate who commits murder : judgements of fact and value in law and social science.* New England Journal on Criminal and Civil Confinement. Boston, MA. 11 : 267-327, 1985, no. 2.

Adam, R. *Die Debatte um die Todesstrafe in den USA erneut aufgelebt (The debate on the death penalty in the U.S.A. is Taken up again).* Kriminalistik. Hamburg. 32 : 321-322, Juli 1977.

Adam, R. *Die Todesstrafe in der Welt (Capital punishment in the world).* Kriminalistik. Hamburg. 26 : 32-34, Januar 1972.

Adamo, S.J. *It's time to outlaw capital punishment.* U.S. Catholic. Chicago, IL. 31 : 19-20, May 1965.

Adams, W. *Capital punishment in Imperial and Soviet criminal law.* American Journal of Comparative Law. Ann Arbor, MI. 18 : 575-594, 1970, no. 3.

Adelstein, R.P. *Informational paradox and the pricing of crime : capital sentencing standards in economic perspective.* Journal of Criminal Law and Criminology. Chicago, IL. 70 : 281-298, 1979.

Adler, S. *The cure that kills.* American Lawyer. New York, N.Y. 7 : 1, 29-33, September 1986.

Adler, S. *Florida's zealous prosecutors : death specialists.* American Lawyer. New York, N.Y. 3 : 35, September 1982.

Alderson, J. *Gaining the peace.* Criminal Law Review. London. 708-718, November 1986.

Alexander, L. *Retributionism and the inadvertent punishment of the innocent.* Law and Philosophy. Dordrecht. 2 : 233-246, 1983.

Alker, H., C. Hosticka and M. Mitchell. *Jury selection as a biased social process.* Law and Society Review. Denver, CO. 9-41, Fall 1976.

Allen, E.J. *Capital punishment : your protection and mine. In* The death penalty in American ; an anthology. Edited by H.A. Bedau. Garden City, N.Y., Anchor Books, 1964, p. 135-146.

Allen, E.J. *A police chief's views on capital punishment. In* Readings in criminology and penology. *By* D. Dressler. New York, N.Y., Columbia University Press, 1964, P. 484-488.

Allison, R. *Difficulties diagnosing the multiple personality syndrome in a death penalty case.* International Journal of Clinical and Experimental Hypnosis. Liverpool, N.Y. 32 : 102-117, 1984.

Alston, J.P. *Japanese and American attitudes toward the abolition of capital punishment.* Criminology. Beverly Hills, CA. 14 : 271-276, 1976, no. 2.

Alvarez Ganoza, P.L. *Origen y trayectoria de la aplicaciòn de la pena de muerte en la historia del derecho peruano, época republicana 1821-1937 y algunos antecedentes coloniales (The origin and evolution of the application of the death penalty in the history of Peruvian law, republican era 1821-1937 and some colonial antecedents).* Lima, 1974, XVI, 207 p.

American Bar Association. *Section of Criminal Law. Pros and cons of capital punishment.* Proceedings. Washington, D.C. 5-25, 24-26, August 1959.

American Civil Liberties Union. *Background paper on the Supreme Court's death penalty decisions.* New York, N.Y., 1976, 12 p.

American Institute of Public Opinion. *Public opinion and the death penalty. In* The death penalty in America ; an anthology. Edited by H.A. Bedau. Garden City, N.Y., Anchor Books, 1964, p. 236-241.

American Law Institute and American Bar Association. *Joint Committee on Continuing Legal Education.* The problem of punishing homicide. Philadelphia, PA., American Law Institute, 1962, 92 p.

American Psychiatric Association. *Position statement on medical participation in capital punishment.* American Journal of Psychiatry. Washington, D.C. 137 : 1487, 1980, no. 11.

Amnesty International. *China : violations of human rights* – Prisoners of conscience and the death penalty in the People's Republic of China. London, 1984.

Amnesty International. *The death penalty.* London, 1979, 209 p.

Amnesty International. *The death penalty. In* Amnesty International Handbook. London, 1983, p. 10-11.

Amnesty International. *The death penalty : no solution to illicit drugs.* London, 1987.

Amnesty International. *The death penalty in Japan* – Report of an Amnesty International mission to Japan 21 February – 3 March 1983. London, 1986.

Amnesty International. *The death penalty in Western Europe.* London, 1986.

Amnesty International. *Declaration of Stockholm. In* Amnesty International Handbook. London, 1983, p. 73-74.

Amnesty International. *Jamaica – The death penalty* – Report of an Amnesty International mission to Jamaica. London, 1984, 63 p.

Amnesty International. *La pena di morte nel mondo.* Convegno inter-

nazionale di Bologna, 28-30 ottobre 1982. Casale Monferrato, Marietti, 1983, 258 p.
Amnesty International. *Proposal for a Presidential Commission on the death penalty in the United States of America. In* The death penalty in America. Edited by H.A. Bedau, 3rd ed. Oxford, Oxford University Press, 1982, p. 375-382.
Amnesty International. *Séminaire sur : peine de mort.* Paris, 18 juin 1977.
Amnesty International. *United States : the death penalty.* London, 1987, 245 p.
Amsterdam, A.G. *Capital punishment. In* The death penalty in America. Edited by H.A. Bedau, 3rd ed. Oxford, Oxford University Press, 1982, p. 346-358.
Amsterdam, A.G. *The case against the death penalty.* Juris Doctor : 11, November 1971.
Anashkin, G.Z. *Smertnaia kazń v kapitalisticheskih gosudarstvah : istpriko-pravovoi ocherk (The death penalty in capitalist countries : an historical and legal outline).* Moscow, 1971.
Ancel, M. *Capital punishment in the second half of the twentieth century.* Review – International Commission of Jurists (Geneva) no. 2 : 33-48, June 1969.
Ancel, M. *Le crime politique et le droit pénal au XXe siècle (The political crime and criminal law in the 20th century).* Revue d'Histoire Politique et Constitutionnelle. Paris : 87, 1938.
Ancel, M. *The death penalty in European countries.* Strasbourg, Council of Europe. European Committee on Crime Problems, 1962, 80 p.
Ancel, M. *Les doctrines de la défense sociale devant le problème de la peine de mort (Social defence doctrine regarding the problem of capital punishment).* Revue de Science Criminelle et de Droit Pénal Comparé. Paris : 404-415, avril-juin 1963.
Ancel, M. *L'exécution de Caryl Chessman et la peine de mort (The execution of Caryl Chessman and the death penalty).* Revue de Science Criminelle et de Droit Pénal Comparé. Paris : 447-456, juillet-septembre 1960.
Ancel, M. *Le problème de la peine de mort (The problem of the death penalty).* Revue de Droit Pénal et de Criminologie. Bruxelles, 44 : 373-393, février 1964.
Ancel, M. *A propos d'une double exécution capitale (Regarding a double execution).* Revue de Science Criminelle et de Droit Pénal Comparé. Paris, 28 : 198-201, janvier-mars 1973.
Ancora *Sull'abolizione della pena di morte in U.S.A. (More on the abolition of the death penalty in the U.S.A.).* Scuola Positiva. Milano 4 : 449-450, 1972, no. 3.
Andenaes, J. *Does punihment deter crime ?* Criminal Law Quarterly (Agincourt, Ont.) 11 : 76-93, November 1968.
Andenaes, J. *General prevention revisited : research and policy implications.* Journal of Criminal Law and Criminology. Baltimore, MD, 66 : 338-365, 1975, no. 3.
Andenaes, J. *The morality of deterrence.* University of Chicago Law Review. Chicago, IL, 37 : 649-664, 1970.

Anders, J. *Should juvenile offenders be sentenced to death ? Punish the guilty*. American Bar Association Journal. Chicago, IL, 72 : 32-35, June 1986.
Anderson, F.W. *Hanging in Canada*. Calgary, Alta, Frontier Publishing Ltd., 1973, 80 p.
Anderson, F.W. *Appeal to United Nations to abolish death penalty*. Amnesty International Newsletter. London, 10 : 6, 1980, no. 1.
Appelbaum, P.S. *Death, the expert witness, and the dangers of going Barefoot. Hospital and Community Psychiatry*. Washington, D.C., 34 : 1003-1004, 1983, no. 1.
Appelbaum, P.S. *Hypotheticals, psychiatric testimony and the death sentence*. Bulletin of American Academy of Psychiatry and Law. 12 : 169-177, 1984.
Appelbaum, P.S. *Psychiatrist's role in the death penalty*. Hospital and Community Psychiatry. Washington, D.C., 32 : 761-762, 1981, no. 11.
Arce Robledo, C. de. *Tribunal de la muerte (The court of death)*. 2nd. ed. Barcelona, 1973, 342 p.
Archer, D., Gartner, R. and Beittel, M. *Homicide and the death penalty : a cross-national test of a deterrence hypothesis*. Journal of Criminal Law and Criminology. Chicago, IL, 74 : 991-1013, 1983, no. 3.
Archer, D., Gartner, R. and Beittel, M. *Violence and crime in a cross-national perspective*. New Haven, Yale University Press, 1984.
Arkin, S.D. *Discrimination and arbitrariness in capital punishment : an analysis of post-Furman murder cases in Dade County,* Florida, 1973-1976. Stanford Law Review, Stanford, CA, 33 : 75-101, 1980, no. 1.
Armitage, A.L. *Rapport de la Commission Royale sur la peine capitale, 1949-1953 (Report of the Royal Commission on the death penalty : 1949-1953)*. Revue de Droit Pénal et de Criminologie. Bruxelles, 574-582, 1954.
Arteaga D. *The death penalty versus thou shalt not kill*. New York, N.Y., Vantage Press, 1980, 143 p.
Aspects juridiques, medicaux et pénitentiaires de la peine incompressible, substitut possible à la peine de mort. Séance de section du 17 décembre 1979 (Legal, medical and correctional aspects of non-commutable punishment as a possible alternative to capital punishment. Court session of 17 December 1979). Revue Pénitentiaire et de Droit Pénal. Paris : 7-23, janvier-mars 1980.
Atholl, J. *Shadow of the gallows*. London, Kohn Long, 1954.
Attribution, salience, and attitudes toward criminal sanctioning. Criminal Justice and Behavior. Beverly Hills, CA, 12 : 305-331.
Aubert, J.M. *Chrétiens et peine de mort (Christians and capital punishment)*. Paris, 1978, 144 p.
Auerbach, S. *Common myths about the death penalty*. Georgia Journal of Corrections. Atlanta, GA, 3 : 41-45, August 1974.
Australia abolishes the death penalty. Quarterly. Camp Hill, PA, 34 : 95, June 1977.
Avio, K.L. *Capital punishment in Canada : a time-series analysis of the deterrent hypothesis*. Canadian Journal of Economics. Toronto, Ont., no. 12 : 647-676, November 1979.

Ayers, J.C. Capital juries and the fait cross-section. Kentucky Law Journal. Lexington, KY, 73 : 1109-1125, 1984/85, no. 4.
Azarian, D. *An examination of the Burger Court and capital punishment : case note on* Barclay v. Florida. Ohio Northern University Law Review.
Ada, OH, 11 : 813-825, 1984.
Bacon, G.R., *ed. Capital punishment.* Prison Journal. Philadelphia, PA, 38 : 34-74, October 1958.
Badinter, R. *L'exécution (The execution).* Paris, 1973, 221 p.
Bailey, R. *Rehabilitation on death row. In The death penalty in America ; an antholoy.* Edited by H.A. Bedau. Garden City, N.Y., Anchor Books, 1964, p. 556-563.
Bailey, W.C. *An analysis of the deterrent effect of the death penalty in North Carolina.* North Carolina Central Law Journal. Durham, N.C., 10 : 29-52, 1978, no. 1.
Bailey, W.C. *Capital punishment and lethal assaults against police.* Criminology. London, 19 : 608-625, 1982, no. 4.
Bailey, W.C., Martin J. and Gray L. *Crime and deterrence : a correlational analysis.* Journal of Research in Crime and Delinquency. Davis, CA, 1é : 124-143, July 1974.
Bailey, W.C. *Deterrence and the celerity of the death penalty : a neglected question in deterrence research.* Madison, WI, University of Wisconsin, 1978, 46 p.
Bailey, W.C. *Deterrence and the death penalty for murder in Utah : a time series analysis.* Journal of Contemporary Law. Salt Lake City, UT, 5 : 1-20, 1978.
Bailey, W.C. *Deterrent effect of capital punishment during the 1950's.* Rockville, MD, NCJRS Microfiche Program, 1978, 47 p.
Bailey, W.C. *Deterrent effect of the death penalty : an extended time series analysis.* Omega, Elmsford, N.Y., 10 : 235-259, 1979-1980, no. 2.
Bailey, W.C. *The deterrent effect of the death penalty for murder in California.* Southern California Law Review. Los Angeles, CA, 52 : 743-764, 1979, no. 3.
Bailey, W.C. *The deterrent effect of the death penalty for murder in Ohio : a time-series analysis.* Cleveland State Law Review, Cleveland, OH, 28 : 51-81, 1979, no. 1.
Bailey, W.C. *Disaggregation in deterrence and death penalty research : the case of murder in Chicago.* Journal of Criminal Law and Criminology. Chicago, IL, 74 : 827-859, 1963, no. 3.
Bailey, W.C. *Imprisonment v. the death penalty as a deterrent to murder.* Law and Human Behavior. New York, N.Y., 1 : 239-260, 1977, no. 3.
Bailey, W.C. *A multivariate cross-sectional and longitudinal analysis of the deterrent effect of the death penalty.* Paper presented at the 1976 annual meeting of the American Society of Criminology. Cleveland, OH, Cleveland State University, 1976, 16 p.
Bailey, W.C. *A multivariate cross-sectional analysis of the deterrent effect of the death penalty.* Sociology and Social Reseach. Los Angeles, CA, 64 : 183-207, 1980, no. 2.

Bailey, W.C. *Murder and capital punishment : some further evidence.* American Journal of Orthopsychiatry. Albany, N.Y., 45 : 669-688, 1975, no. 4. Also in *Capital punishment in the United States.* Edited by H.A. Bedau and C.M. Pierce. New York, N.Y., AMS Press, 1976, p. 314-335.

Bailey, W.C. *Murder and capital punishment in the nation's capital.* Justice Quarterly. Omaha, NE, no. 1/2 : 211-223, 1984.

Bailey, W.C. *Murder and the death penalty.* Journal of Criminal Law and Criminology. Baltimore, MD, 65 : 416-423, September 1974.

Bailey, W.C. *Rape and the death penalty : a neglected area of deterrence research. In Capital punishment in the United States.* Edited by H.A. Bedau and C.M. Pierce. New York, N.Y., AMS Press, 1976, p. 336-358.

Bailey, W.C. *Some further evidence on imprisonment vs. the death penalty as a deterrent to murder.* Law and Human Behavior. New York, N.Y., 2 : 245-260, 1978, no. 3.

Bailey, W.C. *Use of the death penalty v. outrage at murder : some additional evidence and considerations.* Crime and Delinquency. Hackensack, N.J., 22 : 31-39, January 1976, no. 1.

Baker, W.G. *The death penalty – The alternatives after.* Furman v. Georgia. Albany Law Review. Albany, N.Y., 37 : 344-364, 1973.

Balás, O. *Ukládáni trestu smrti (Sentencing to death).* Socialicka Zakonnost. Prague : 307-311, 1970, no. 5.

Baldus, D.C., Pulaski C. and Woodworth G. *Arbitrariness and discrimination in the administration of the death penalty.* Stetson Law Review (Petersburg, FE, 15 : 133-261, 1986.

Baldus, D.C., Pulaski C. and Woodworth G. *Comparative review of death sentences : an empirical study of the Georgia experience.* Journal of Criminal Law and Criminology. Chicago, IL, 74 : 661-753, 1983, no. 3.

Baldus, D.C. and Cole J. *A comparison of the work of Thorsten Sellin and Isaac Ehrlich on the deterrent effect of capital punishment.* Yale Law Journal, New Haven, CT, 85 : 170-186, 1975.

Baldus, D.C., Pulaski C. and Woodworth G. *Identifying comparatively excessive sentences of death : a quantitative approach.* Stanford Law Review. Stanford, CA, 33 : 1-74, 1980.

Baldus, D.C., Pulaski C. and Woodworth G. *Monitoring and evaluating contemporary death sentencing systems : lessons from Georgia.* University of California Davis Law Review. Davis, CA, 18 : 1375-1408, 1985.

Ball, J. *The deterrence concept in criminology and law.* Journal of Criminal Law, Criminology and Police Science. Baltimore, MD, no. 46 : 347-354, September-October 1955.

Balogh, J.K. and Green J.D. *Capital punishment : some reflections. Federal Probation.* Washington, D.C., 30 : 24-27, December 1966.

Bamonte, T. *Una disputa medioevale sulla pena di morte (A medieval dispute on the death penalty).* Rassegna di Studi Penitenziari. Roma, 188-201, 1954.

Baratta, A. *Aspetti extragiudiziali della pena di morte (Extra judicial aspects of the death penalty).* In La pena di morte nel mondo. By Amnesty International. Casale Monferrato, Marietti, 1983, p. 175.

Barber, P.G. People v. Smith : *Mandatory death laid to rest.* Albany Law Review. Albany, N.Y., 49 : 926-966, 1985, no. 4.

Baber, R. N. and Wilson P.R. *Deterrent aspect of capital punishment and its effect on conviction rates : the Queensland experience.* Australian and New Zealand Journal of Criminology. Melbourne, 1 : 100-108, 1968, no. 2.
Barbero Santos, M. *La peine de mort en Espagne : histoire de son abolition (The death penalty in Spain : the story of its abolition).* In Mélanges en l'honneur du Doyen Pierre Bouzat. Paris, éditions A. Pedone, 1980, p. 103-116.
Barbero Santos, M. *Pena de muerte : el ocaso de un mito (Death penalty : sunset of a myth).* Buenos Aires, Ediciones Depalma, 1985, 273 p.
Barbero Santos, M. *Postulats politico-criminels du système répressif espagnol en vigueur (Political and criminalistic bases of the present Spanish criminal system.* Revue de Science Criminelle et de Droit Pénal Comparé. Paris, 30 : 633-651, juillet-septembre 1975.
Barfield, W. *Woman on death row.* Nashville, TN, Oliver Nelson Books, 1985.
Barnett, A. *Crime and capital punishment : some recent studies.* Journal of Criminal Justice. New York, N.Y., 6 : 291-303, 1978, no. 4.
Barnett, A. *The deterrent effect of capital punishment : a test of some recent studies.* Operations Research. Baltimore, MD, 29 : 346-370, 1981, no. 2.
Barnett, A. *Some disturbing patterns for the Georgia death sentence.* University of California Davis Law Review. Davis, CA, 18 : 1327-1374, 1985.
Barnhill, D.S. *Administering the death penalty.* Washington and Lee Law Review. Lexington, WA, 39 : 101-124, 1982, no. 1.
Barrett Jr., E.L. *Anderson and the judicial function.* Southern California Law Review. Los Angeles, CA, 45 : 739-749, 1972, no. 3.
Barring, L. *Goetterspruch und Henkernand. Die Todesstrafen in der Geschichte der Menschheit (God's sentence and the executioner's hand. The death penalty in the history of menkind).* Bergisch-Gladback, Gustav Luebbe Verlag, 1967.
Barrows, S.J. *Legislative tendencies as to capital punishment.* Annals of the American Academy of Political and Social Science. Philadelphia, PA, 29 : 618-621, May 1907.
Barry, J.V. *Hanged by the neck until...* Sydney Law Review. Sydney, 2 : 401-413, March 1958.
Barry, R.V. Furman to Gregg : *The judicial and legislative history.* Howard Law Journal. Washington, D.C., 22 : 53-117, 1979, no. 1.
Mr. Barzun and capital punishment. *Crime and Delinquency.* Hackensack, N.J., 15 : 28-42, 1969, no. 1.
Mr. Barzun and capital punishment : comments on Jacques Barzun's article " *In favor of capital punishment* "... American Scholar. Washington, D.C., 31 : 436-447, Summer 1962.
Barzun, J. *In favor of capital punishment. In* The death penalty in America ; an anthology. Edited by H.A. Bedau. Garden City, N.Y., Anchor Books, 1964, p. 154-165.
Bassiouni, M.C., Lahey, K.A. and Sang L.M. *La peine de mort aux Etats-Unis. L'état de la question en 1972 (Capital punishment in the United States. Status of the problem in 1972).* Revue de Science Criminelle et de Droit Pénal Comparé. Paris, 28 : 23-43, janvier-mars 1973.
Bastard or legitimate child of Furman ? *An Analysis of Wyoming's new*

capital punishment law. Land and Water Law Review. Laramie, WY, 9 : 209-236, 1974.

Batey, B. *Federal habeas corpus relief and the death penalty : finality with a capital F.* University of Florida Law Review. Gainesville, FL, 36 : 252-272, 1984, no. 2.

Battiati, A. *Il problema della pena di morte nell'Italia d'oggi (The problem of capital punishment in Italy today).* Rassegna Penitenziaria e Criminologia. Roma, no. 3/4 : 569-610, 1982.

Baumann, J. *La politique criminelle dans l'état de droit social (à l'occasion d'un livre de M. Wuertenberger).* Revue de Science Criminelle et de Droit Pénal Comparé. Paris, 27 : 851-857, octobre-décembre 1972.

Baumann, L. *Ceux qu'on n'a pas exécutés (la vie aux îles du salut des condamnés à morts graciés) (Those who were not executed ; life in the health islands of those pardoned).* Archives d'anthropologie Criminelle et de Criminologie. Paris, 188-193, 1909.

Bavcon, L. *Prispevek k razpravam o smrtni kazni (Continuation of the debate on capital punishment).* Pravnik. Ljubljana : 155-162, 1979, no. 4/6.

Bayer, R. *Lethal injections and capital punishment : medicine in service of the state.* Journal of Prison and Jail Health. New York, N.Y., 4 : 7-15, 1984.

Bayer, V. *O problemu smrtne kazne u nas danas (On the problem of the death penalty today).* Nasa Zakonistot, Zagreb, 28 : 137-145, 1974, no. 2.

Beattie, J.M. *Attitudes towards crime and punishment in Upper Canada, 1830-1850 :* a documentary study. Toronto, Ont., Centre of Criminology, University of Toronto, 1977, 174 p.

Beccaria, C. *Dei delitti e delle pene (On crimes and punishments).* (Reprint of 1764 ed.). Milano, Giuffrè, 1964. 136 p.

Beccaria, C. *On crimes and punishment, translated by H. Paolucci.* Indianapolis, IN, Bobbs-Merrill Company, 1983, 99 p.

Beccaria, C. *Traité des délits et des peines (Essay on crimes and punishments).* Translated by Defat. Paris, Dalibon, 1822.

Bedau, H.A. *Are mandatory capital sentences inherently discriminatory ?* Jewish Advocate. Boston, MA, 22 : 1, May 1975.

Bedau, H.A. *Bentham's utilitarian critique of the death penalty.* Journal of Criminal Law and Criminology. Chicago, IL, 74 : 1033-1065, 1983, no. 3.

Bedau, H.A. *Capital punishment.* Prison Journal. Philadelphia, PA, 34-74, October 1958.

Bedau, H.A. *Capital punishment in Oregon, 1903-1964.* Oregon Law Review. Eugene, OR, 45 : 1-39, December 1965.

Bedau, H.A. *Capital punishment in the United States.* Howard Law Journal. Washington, D.C., 10 : 225-233, 1960.

Bedau, H.A. and Pierce, C.M., eds. *Capital punishment in the United States.* New York, N.Y., AMS Press, 1976, 567 p.

Bedau, H.A. *The case against the death penalty.* New York, N.Y. American Civil Liberties Union, 1984.

Bedau, H.A. *Challenging the death penalty.* Harvard Civil Rights – Civil Liberties Law Review. Cambridge, MA, 9 : 624-643, May 1974.

Bedau, H.A. *The courts, the constitution, and capital punishment.* Lexington, MA, D.C. Heath and Co., 1977.

Bedau, H.A. *Death as a punishment. In* The death penalty in America ; an anthology. Edited by H.A. Bedau. Garden City, N.Y., Anchor Books, 1964, p. 214-231.

Bedau, H.A. *Death is different : studies in the morality, law and politics of capital punishment.* Boston, MA, Northeastern University Press, 1987, 300 p.

Bedau, H.A. *The death penalty ; social policy and social justice.* Arizona State Law Journal. Tempe, AZ, 767-802, 1977, no. 4.

Bedau, H.A. *The death penalty and state constitutional rights in the United States of America.* Crime Prevention and Criminal Justice Newsletter. Vienna, no. 12/13 : 19-24, November 1986.

Bedau, H.A. *The death penalty as a deterrent : argument and evidence.* Ethics. Chicago, IL, 80 : 205-217, 1970, no. 3.

Bedau, H.A. *The death penalty in America ; an anthology.* Garden City, N.Y., Anchor Books, 1964, 584 p.

Bedau, H.A. ed. *The death penalty in America.* 3rd ed. Oxford. Oxford University Press, 1982, 424 p.

Bedau, H.A. *The death penalty in America : review and forecast.* Federal Probation. Washington, D.C., 35 : 32-43, June 1971.

Bedau, H.A. *The death penalty today.* Chistian Century. Chicago, IL, 76 : 320-322, 18 March 1959.

Bedau, H.A. *Death sentences in New Jersey 1907-1960.* Rutgers Law Review. Newark, N.J., 19 : 1-54, Fall 1964.

Bedau, H.A. *Deterrence and the death penalty : a reconsideration.* Journal of Criminal Law, Criminology and Police Science. Baltimore, MD, 61 : 539-548, December 1970.

Bedau, H.A. *Felony, murder, rape and the mandatory death penalty ; a study in discretionary justice.* Suffolk University Law Review. Boston, MA, 10 : 493-520, Spring 1976. Also in Capital punishment in the United States. Edited by H.A. Bedau and C.M. Pierce. New York, N.Y., AMS Press, 1975, p. 54-75.

Bedau, H.A. *Furman's wake in the land of bean and cod.* Prison Journal. Philadelphia, PA, 53 : 4-18, Spring-Summer 1973.

Bedau, H.A. *The future of capital punishment.* Project statement submitted to the Russel Sage Foundation. New York, N.Y., 1973.

Bedau, H.A. *Gregg v. Georgia and the new death penalty.* Criminal Justice Ethics. New York, N.Y., 4 : 3-17, 1985.

Bedau, H.A. *The issue of capital punishment.* Current History. Philadelphia, PA, 53 : 82-87, 1967, no. 312.

Bedau, H.A. and Radelet, M.L. *Miscarriages of justice in potentially capital cases.* New York, N.Y., American Civil Liberties Union, 1985. Stanford Law Review. Stanford, CA, 39 : July 1987.

Bedau, H.A. *Murder, errors of justice, and capital punishment. In* The death penalty in America ; an anthology. Eddited by H.A. Bedau. Garden City, N.Y., Anchor Books, 1964, p. 434-452.

Bedau, H.A. *The 1964 death penalty referendum in Oregon. Some notes*

from a participant-observer. Crime and Delinquency. Hackensack, N.J., 26 : 528-536, 1980, no. 4.
Bedau, H.A. *The Nixon administration and the deterrent effect of the death penalty.* University of Pittsburgh Law Review. Pittsburgh, PA, 34 : 557-566, Summer 1973.
Bedau, H.A. *Offenses punishable by death. In* The death penalty in America ; an anthology. Edited by H.A. Bedau. Garden City, N.Y. Anchor Books, 1964, p. 39-52.
Bedau, H.A. *Parole of capital offenders, recidivism, and life imprisonment. In* The death penalty in America ; an anthology. Edited by H.A. Bedau. Garden City, N.Y., Anchor Books, 1964, p. 395-405.
Bedau, H.A. *The politics of death.* Trial. Washington, D.C., 8 : 44-46, 1972, no. 2.
Bedau, H.A. *Retribution and the theory of punishment.* Journal of Philosophy. New York, N.Y., 55 : 601-620, 1978.
Bedau, H.A. *A social philosopher looks at the death penalty.* American Journal of Psychiatry. Washington, D.C., 123 : 1361-1370, 1967.
Bedau, H.A. *Social science research in the aftermath of Furman v. Georgia : creating new knowledge about capital punishment in the United States. In* Issues in criminal justice : planning and evaluation. Edited by M. Riedel and D. Chappell. New York, N.Y., Praeger Publishers, 1976, p. 75-86.
Bedau, H.A. *The struggle over capital punishment in New Jersey. In* The death penalty in America ; an anthology. Edited by H.A. Bedau. Garden City, N.Y., Anchor Books, 1964, p. 374-395.
Bedau, H.A. *A survey of the debate on capital punishment in Canada, England and the United States, 1948-1958.* Prison Journal. Philadelphia, PA, 38 : 35-40, October 1958.
Bedau, H.A. *Thinking of the death penalty as cruel and unusual punishment.* University of California Davis Law Review. Davis, CA, 18 : 873-926, 1985.
Bedau, H.A. *Toward a comparative jurisprudence on capital punishment.* Harvard Civil Rights - Civil Liberties Review. Cambridge, MA, 19 : 235-243, 1984, no. 1.
Bedau, H.A. *Volume and rate of capital punishment. In* The death penalty in America ; an anthology. Edited by H.A. Bedau. Garden City, N.Y., Anchor Books, 1964, p. 56-74.
Beggs, T. *The deterrent influence of capital punishment.* Transactions of the National Association for the Promotion of Social Science. London, 213, 1865.
Begley, W.F. *The aggravating circumstance of Arizona's death penalty statute : a review.* Arizona Law Review. Tucson, AZ, 26 : 661-680, 1984, no. 3.
Beichman, A. *The first electrocution.* Commentary. New York, N.Y., 35 : 410-419, May 1963.
Beman, L.T. ed. *Selected articles on capital punishment.* New York, N.Y., The H.W. Wilson Co., 1925, 336 p.
Bennet, J.A. *historic move : Delaware abolishes capital punishment.* American Bar Association Journal. Chicago, IL, 44 : 1053, 1958.
Bensing, R. and Schroeder O. *Homicide in an urban community.* Springfield, IL, Charles C. Thomas, 1960.

Bentham, J. *The rational of punishment.* London, 1830.

Bentham, J. *Théorie des peines et des récompenses, redigée en français d'après les manuscrits par E. Dumont (Theory on punishments and rewards, written in French from his manuscripts by E. Dumont).* 3e ed. Paris, Bossange, 1826.

Berard, A. *La publicité des exécutions capitales (Publicity and executions).* Archives d'Anthropologie Criminelle et de Criminologie. Paris, 121-134, 1894.

Berger, R. *Death penalties : the Supreme Court's obstacle course.* Cambridge, MA, Harvard University Press, 1982, 242 p.

Berger, R. and Bedau, H. *A crusading philosopher goes overboard. Ohio State Law Journal.* Columbus, OH, 45 : 863-881, 1984, no. 4.

Bergwerk, R. *Step toward uniformity : review of life sentences in capital cases.* Florida State University Law Review. Tallahassee, FL, 6 : 1015-1027, 1978, no. 3.

Beristain, A. *Katholizismus and Todesstrafe (Catholicism and the death penalty).* Zeitschrift fuer die gesamte Strafrechtswissenschaft. Berlin, B.D.R., 89 : 215-238, 1977, no. 1.

Beristain, A. *El catolicismo ante la pena de muerte (Catholicism faced with the death penalty). In* La pena de muerte, seis repuestas. Madrid, Boletin Oficial del Estado, 1978.

Berkson, L.C. *The concept of cruel and unusual punishment.* Lexington, MA, Lexington Books, 1975, 252 p.

Berman, D.L. *A selected bibliography on capital punishment.* Conference on World Abolition of Capital Punishment. Stockholm, Amnesty International, December 1977, 111 p.

Bernard, J.L. and Dwyer W.O. *Witherspoon v. Illinois : the court was right.* Law and Psychology Review. University, AL, 8 : 105-114, Spring 1984.

Berns, W. *Defending the death penalty.* Crime and Delinquency. Hackensack, N.J., 26 : 503-511, 1980, no. 4.

Berns, W. *For capital punishment : crime and the morality of the death penalty.* New York, N.Y., Basic Books, 1979.

Berns, W. *The morality of anger. In* The death penalty in America. Edited by H.A. Bedau, 3rd ed. Oxford. Oxford University Press, 1982, p. 333-341.

Berry, J. *My experience as an executioner.* Edited by H. Snowden Ward (reprint of 1892 ed.). Detroit, MI, Gale Research Co., 1972, 148 p.

Bertran, L. *Sobre la perduracion de la ignominiosa pena de muerte (On maintaining the shameful death penalty). In* Actes du IIe Congrès International de Criminologie. Vol. 4. Paris, Presses Universitaires, 1953, p. 596-599.

Bessette, J.-M. *Il était une fois... la guillotine (Once upon a time... the guillotine).* Paris, éd. Alternatives, 1982, 126 p.

Beyleveld, D. *A bibliography on general deterrence research.* Westmead. Saxon House, 1980.

Beyleveld, D. *Deterrence research as a basis for deterrence policies.* Howard Journal of Penology and Crime Prevention. Sheffield, 18 : 135-149, 1979, no. 3.

Beyleveld, D. *Ehrlich's analysis of deterrence. Methodological strategy and*

ethics in Isaac Ehrmich's research and writing on the death penalty as a deterrent. British Journal of Criminology. Croydon, Surrey, 22 : 101-123, 1982, no. 2.
Bhattacharyya, S.K. *Capital punishment Social Defence.* New Delhi, 17 : 25-34, 1982, no. 67.
Bice, S.H. *Anderson and the adequate state ground.* Southern California Law Review. Los Angeles, CA, 45 : 750-766, 1972, no. 3.
Biddy, R.W. *Project Canada : an examination of the public perception of social problems, law and deviance in Canada.* Ottawa, Ont., Ministry of Solicitor General, 1976.
Bishop, T. and Martin A. *Statutory aggravating circumstances and the death penalty : what lies beyond the threshold of Zant v. Stephens ?* Mercer Law Review. Macon, GA, 35 : 1443-1468, 1984.
Black, C.L. *Capital punishment : the inevitability of caprice and mistake.* 2nd. ed. New York, N.Y., W.W. Norton and Company, Inc., 1981, 174 p.
Black, C.L. *Crisis in capital punishment.* Maryland Law Review. Baltimore, MD, 31 : 289, 1971.
Black, C.L. *The death penalty now.* Tulane Law Review. New Orleans, LA : 51, 1977, no. 3.
Black, C.L. *Death sentences and our criminal justice system. In* The death penalty in America. Edited by H.A. Bedau, 3rd ed. Oxford. Oxford University Press, 1982, p. 359-363.
Black, C.L. *Objections to S. 1382, a bill to establish rational criteria for the imposition of capital punishment.* Crime and Delinquency. Hackensack, N.J., 26 : 441-452, 1980, no. 4.
Black, C.L. *Reflections on opposing the penalty of death.* St. Mary's Law Journal. San Antonio, TX, 10 : 1-12, 1978, no. 1.
Black, T. and Orsagh, T. *New evidence on the efficacy of sanctions as a deterrent to homicide.* Social Science Quarterly. Austin, TX, 58 : 616-631, 1978, no. 4.
Blackie, D.K. *What does the Bible say about capital punishment.* Church Herald. Grand Rapids, MI, 18 : 5, 21 April 1961.
Blackshield, A.R. Capital punishment in India. Indian Law Institute Journal. New Delhi, 21 : 137-226, 1979, no. 2.
Blake, L. *The sentence for murder : the case for retribution.* New Law Journal. London : 914-1058, 1973.
Bland, J. *The common hangman : English and Scottish hangmen before the abolition of common executions.* Colchester, Essex, Ian Henry, 1984, 174 p.
Block, E.B. *And may God have mercy : the case againts capital punishment.* San Francisco, CA, Fearon Publishers, 1962, 197 p.
Block, E.B. *When men play god : the fallacy of capital punishment.* San Francisco, CA, Cragmont Publishers, 1983, 205 p.
Blom-Cooper, *L. Good Moral reasons. In* The hanging question. Edited by L. Blom-Cooper. London, Duckworth and Co., 1969, 138 p.
Blom-Cooper, L. ed. *The hanging question. Essays on the death penalty.* London, Duckworth and Co., 1969, 138 p.
Blom-Cooper, L. *The penalty for murder.* British Journal of Criminology. London, 13 : 188-190. April 1973.

Bluestone, H. and McGehee E.G. *Reaction to extreme stress : impending death by execution.* American Journal of Psychiatry. Washington, D.C., 119 : 393-396, November 1962.

Blumstein, A., Cohen J. and Nagin D., eds. *Deterrence and incapacitation : estimating the effects of criminal sanctions on crime rates.* Washington, D.C., National Academy of Sciences, 1978, 431 p.

Boaz, J.E. *Summary process and the rule of law : expediting death penalty cases in the federal courts.* Yale Law Journal. New Haven, CT, 94 : 349-370, 1985.

Bobbio, N. *Il dibattito attuale sulla pena di morte (Today's debate on capital punishment). In* La pena di morte nel mondo. By Amnesty International. Casale Monferrato, Marietti, 1983, p. 13-32.

Bockle, H. and Pohiers J. *The death penalty and torture.* New York, The Seabury Press, 1979.

Boehm, V. *Mr. Prejudice, Miss Sympathy and the authoritarian personality : an application of psychological measuring techniques to the problem of jury bias.* Wisconsin Law Review. Madison, WI : 734-800, 1968.

Bolle, P.H. *Abolition of the death penalty : dream or reality !* Crime Prevention and Criminal Justice Newsletter. Vienna, no. 12/13 : 47-50, November 1986.

Bonneville de Marsangy, A. *De l'amélioration de la loi criminelle (On the improvement of criminal law).* Paris, Librairie Générale de Jurisprudence, 1864.

Bonnie, R.J. *Psychiatry and the death penalty : emerging problems in Virginia.* Virginia Law Review. Charlottesville, VA, 66 : 167-189, 1980, no. 2.

Borchard, E.M. *Convicting the innocent : sixty-five actual errors of criminal justice.* New York, N.Y., Da Capo Press Inc., 1932.

Borowitz, A.I. *Under sentence of death – Is the death penalty a deterrent to crime ? The literature of capital punishment is a primary source to be considered.* American Bar Association Journal. Chicago, IL, no. 64 : 1259-1266, 1978.

Bottoms, A.E. and Rutherford, A.F. *The treatment of offenders ; capital and corporal punishment. In* Use of criminology literature. Edited by M. Wright. London, Butterworth and Co. Ltd., 1974, p. 143-144.

Bouzat, P. *Le problème de la peine de mort (The problem of capital punishment).* Bulletin de la Société Internationale de Criminologie. Paris, 35-42, 1953, 1er et 2e semestres.

Bouzat, P. *Why am I still an advocate of the death penalty ?* Zbornik Pravnog Fakulteta v Zagreba. Zagreb, 289 : 331-339, 1978, no. 3/4.

Bower, B. *Testimony on dangerousness ruled admissible.* Psychiatric News. Washington, D.C., 18 : 1-17, 1983, no. 15.

Bowers, W.J. and Pierce, G.L. *Arbitrariness and discrimination under post-Furman capital statuts.* Crime and Delinquency. Hackensack, N.J., 26 : 563-635, 1980, no. 4.

Bowers, W.J. and Pierce, G.L. *Deterrence or brutalization : what is the effect of executions ?* Crime and Delinquency. Hackensack, N.J., 26 : 453-484, 1980, no. 4.

Bowers, W.J. and Pierce, G.L. *Executions in America.* Lexington, MA, Lexington Books, 1974, 528 p.

Bowers, W.J. and Pierce, G.L. *The illusion of deterrence : a critique of Isaac Enrlich's research on capital punishment.* Yale Law Journal. New Haven, CT, 85, 1976, no. 2.

Bowers, W.J. and Pierce, G.L. *The illusion of deterrence in Isaac Ehrlich's research on capital punishment.* Yale Law Journal. New Haven, CT, 16 : 187-208, December 1975. Also in Capital punishment in the United States. Edited by H.A. Bedau and C.M. Pierce, New York, N.Y. AMS Press, 1976, p. 372-395.

Bowers, W.J. and McDevitt, J.F. *Legal homicide : death as punishment in America 1864-1982.* Boston, MA, Northeastern University Press, 1984, 632 p.

Bowers, W.J. *The pervasiveness of arbitrariness and discrimination under post-Furman capital statutes.* Journal of Criminal Law and Criminology. Chicago, IL, 74 : 1067-1100, 1983, no. 3.

Bowers, W.J. and Pierce, G.L. *Racial discrimination and criminal homicide under post-Furman capital statutes.* In The death penalty in America. Edited by H.A. Bedau, 3rd ed. Oxford. Oxford University Press, 1982, p. 206-223.

Boyd, J. and Logue, J. *Developments in the application of Florida's capital sentencing law.* University of Miami Law Review. Miami, FL, 34 : 441-497, 1980.

Boyles, W.J. and McPheters L.R. *Capital punishment as a deterrent to violent crime : cross section evidence.* Journal of Behavioral Economics. Macomb, IL. 6 : 67-86, 1977.

Bradley, L. *The impact of a sliding-scale approach to due process on capital punishment litigation.* Syracuse Law Review. Syracuse, N.Y., 30 : 675-703, 1979, no. 2.

Branca, A.E. *Capital punishment.* Chitty's Law Journal. Peterborough, Ont., 24 : 37-43, 1976, no. 2.

Brasfield, P. and Elliot, J.M. *Deathman pass me by : two years on death row.* San Bernardino, CA. Borgo Books, 1982.

Brauchli, C. *From the wool-sack.* Colorado Lawyer, 15 : 428, 1986.

Brewster, C.R. *The Georgia death penalty statute – is it constitutional, even after revision ?* Georgia Journal of Corrections. Atlanta, GA, 3 : 14-19, Winter, 1974.

Bridge F. and Mosure J. *Capital punishment : staff research, report no. 26.* Columbus, OH, Ohio Legislature Service Committee, 1961.

Briel, S. *An innocent man on death row.* American Lawyer. New York, N.Y., 5 : 1, December 1983.

Bright, S. Inconsistent in doling out death. National Prison Project Journal. Washington, 6 : 12-15, 1985.

Brinkman, B.S. *The presumption of life : a starting point for a due process analysis of capital punishment.* Yale Law Journal. New Haven, CT, 94 : 351-373, 1984, no. 2.

Britain abolishes the death penalty. Federal Probation. Washington, D.C., 34 : 78, March 1970.

Brocklebank-Fowler, C. *A pointless execution. In* The hanging question.

Edited by L. Blom-Cooper. London, Duckworth and Co., 1969, p. 67-72.
Broda, C. *Plaidoyer pour l'abolition de la peine de mort (Address for the abolition of capital punishment).* Forum, Conseil de l'Europe, Strasbourg, no. 4 : 11-12, 1978.
Brody, R. *Don't kill children.* American Bar Association Journal. Chicago, IL, 72 : 32, June 1986.
Bronson, E.J. *On the conviction proneness and representativeness of the death qualified jury : an empirical study of Colorado veniremen.* University of Colorado Law Review. Boulder, CO, 42 : 1-33, 1970, no. 1.
Brown, C.R. *Gary Gilmore's date with the executioner.* Quarterly Journal of Corrections. Memphis, TN, 1 : 6-31, 1977, no. 2.
Brown, E.G. *Let's take another look.* Peace Officers Association of the State of California. Fresno, CA, 5 : 4, March-April 1955.
Brown, E.G. *Message to the Legislature to the abolition of the death penalty.* Californian. San Francisco, CA, 1 : 1-12, May 1960.
Brown, E.G. *Statement... on capital punishment.* Transmitted to the California Legislature 31 January 1963. Sacramento, CA, State of California, 1963, 8 p.
Brown, W. *Women who died in the chair.* London, Collier, 1963, 183 p.
Browning, J.R. *New death penalty statutes : perpetuating a costly myth.* Gonzaga Law Review. Spokane, WA, 9 : 651-705, Spring 1974.
Bruck, D. *The four men Strom Thurmond sent to the chair.* New York, N.Y., NAACP Legal Defense and Educational Fund, Inc., 1981.
Brudner, A. *Retributivism and the death penalty.* University of Toronto Law Journal. Toronto, Ont., 30 : 337-355, 1980, no. 4.
Bruening, W.H. *The death penalty and the U.S. Supreme Court.* Archiv fuer Recht – und Sozial Philosophie. Wiesbaden, 61 : 387-412, 1975, no. 3.
Buchler, M. *Is capital punishment justified ?* Penal Reform News/Strafhervormingsnuus. Pretoria, no. 62 : 4-9, April 1963.
Bueno Arus, F. *Extradición y pena de muerte en el ordinamiento juridico espanol (Extradition and capital punishment in Spanish law).* Anuario de Derecho Penal y Ciencias Penales. Madrid, 34 : 399-412, 1981, no. 2/3.
Buffard, S. *Fonction sociologique de la peine de mort (The sociological function of capital punishment).* Bulletin de Médecine Légale et de Toxicologie Médicale. Lyon, 15 : 288-291, 1972, no. 5.
Buffum, P.C. *Prison killings and death penalty legislation.* Prison Journal. Philadelphia, PA, 53 : 49-57, Spring-Summer, 1973.
Burkhout, R. and Baker E. *Jurors attitudes and the death penalty.* Social Action and the Law. Brooklyn, N.Y., 3 : 80-81, 1977.
Burnett, C. *Nolo contendere : efficient and effective administration of justice.* Criminal Law Bulletin. Boston, MA, 23 : 117-134, March-April 1987.
Buteler, P. *Inconstitucionalidad de la pena de muerte (The death penalty is unconstitutional).* Revista de la Direction de Asuntos Penales. Mendoza, Argentina, no. 4 : 53-66, 1982.
Bye, R.T. *Capital punishment in the United States.* Philadelphia, PA, Committee of Philanthropic Labor. Yearly Meeting of Friends, 1919.
Caldwell, R.G. *Why is the death penalty retained ?* Annals of the Ameri-

can Academy of Political and Social Science. Philadelphia, PA, no. 284 : 45-54, November 1952.
Callandraud, G.J. *De l'exécution capitale à travers les civilisations et les âges (Capital punishment throughout the civilisation and ages).* Document, Paris, 1979, 233 p.
Callans, P.J. *Sixth amendment : asemblying a jury willing to impose the death penalty : a new disregard for a capital defendant's rights.* Wainwright v. Witt 105S. CT. 844 (1985). Journal of Criminal Law and Criminology. Chicago, IL, 76 : 1027-1105, Winter 1985.
Calvert, E.R. *Capital punishment in the twentieth century.* 5th rev. ed. New York, N.Y., G.P. Putnam's Sons, 1936, 236 p.
Calvert, E.R. *The death penalty enquiry : being a review of the evidence before the Select Committee on Capital Punishment.* Montclair, N.J., Patterson Smith Publishing Corporation, 1973.
Campion, D.R. *Attitudes of state police toward the death penalty. In* The death penalty in America ; an anthology. Edited by H.A. Bedau. Garden City, N.Y., Anchor Books, 1964, p. 252-258.
Campion, D.R. *Does the death penalty protect state police. In* The death penalty in America ; an anthology. Edited by H.A. Bedau. Garden City, N.Y., Anchor Books, 1964, p. 301-314.
Campion, D.R. *The state police and death penalty.* In Minutes of the proceedings and evidence, by the Joint Committee of the Senate and the House of Commons on Capital Punishment. Ottawa, Ont., Queen's Printer, 1955, p. 729-741.
Camus, A. *Réflexions sur la guillotine (Reflections on the guillotine) 1957. In* Essais. By A. Camus. Paris, Gallimard, 1984, p. 1019-1064.
Camus, A. and Koestler, A. *Réflexions sur la peine capitale (Reflections on the death penalty).* Paris, Calmann-Lévy, 1957.
Canada. *Department of the Solicitor General. Capital punishment – new material :* 1965-1972. Ottawa, Ont., Information Canada, 1972, 161 p.
Canada. *The prevention and control of violent crime in Canada.* Ottawa, Ont., March 1975.
Canada. *Department of the Solicitor General.* Questions and answers relating to the capital punishment issue. Ottawa, Ont., 1976.
Canada. *Joint Committee of the Senate and the House of Commons on Capital and Corporal Punishment and Lotteries.* Minutes of Proceedings and Evidence. Appendix F. Ottawa, Ont., Queen's Printer, 1955.
Canada. Report, Ottawa, Ont., Queen's Printer, 1956.
Canada. *Minister of Justice.* Capital punishment ; material relating to its purpose and value. Ottawa, Ont. Queen's Printer, June 1965.
Canadian Association of Chiefs of Police. *Capital punishment : the point of view of the Canadian Association of Chiefs of Police.* Crime et/and Justice. Ottawa, Ont., 4 : 54/67, May 1976.
Canadian Criminology and Corrections Association. *The death penalty – An official statement of policy.* Ottawa, Ont., November 1972, 4 p.
Cannat, P. *A propos du problème de la guillotine (On the problem of the guillotine).* Revue de Science Criminelle et de Droit Pénal Comparé. Paris : 428-429, avril-juin 1974.
Cannat, P. *Peut-il exister une peine de remplacement de la peine de mort ?*

(Is it possible to find an alternative punishment to the death penalty ?) Revue de Science Criminelle et de Droit Pénal. Paris : 477-479, 1967.
Capital punishment. Annals of the American Academy of Political and Social Science. (Philadelphia, PA), November 1952.
Capital punishment. Corrections Compendium. Lincoln, NE, 7 : 8-10, 1983, no. 1.
Capital punishment. Crime Prevention and Criminal Justice Newsletter. Vienna. Special combined issue. November 1986, 67 p.
Capital punishment. Journal of Criminal Law and Criminology. Baltimore, MD, 68 : 601-612, 1977, no. 4.
Capital punishment. Review – International Commission of Jurists. Geneva : 3, April-June 1971.
Capital punishment : a selected bibliography. New York, N.Y., Citizens against Legalized Murder Inc., 1972, 45 p.
Capital punishment : Gregg v. Georgia, Proffitt v. Florida, Jurek v. Texas, Woodson v. North Carolina, Roberts v. Louisiana. Journal of Criminal Law and Criminology. Baltimore, MD, 67 : 437-449, December 1976.
Capital punishment : on the way out ? University of Baltimore Law Review. Baltimore, MD, 1 : 28-48, 1971.
Capital punishment : positions and opinion. Georgia Journal of Corrections. Atlanta, GA, 3 : 26-40, August 1974.
Capital punishment : special selection of data from the social sciences. American Journal of Orthopsychiatry. Albany, N.Y., July 1975.
Capital punishment : trends throughout the world. Crime, Punishment and Correction/Misdaad, Straf en Hervorming. Cape Town, 2 : 72-75, October 1973.
Capital punishment : what the religious community says. Washington, D.C., United Methodist Church, 1978.
Capital punishment abolished. National Council on Crime and Delinquency News. Paramus, N.J., 48 : 11, 1969, no. 5
Capital punishment after Furman. Journal of Criminal Law and Criminology. Baltimore, MD, 64 : 281-289, September 1973.
Capital punishment for juvenile crimes : U.S.A. disregards international standards. International Children's Rights Monitor. Geneva, 2 : 20, 1985, no. 4.
Capital punishment held unconstitutional in California. Review - International Commission of Jurists. Geneva : 63, June 1972.
Capital punishment in the United States. Crime and Delinquency. Hackensack, N.J., no. 4 : 26, 1980.
Capital punishment in Virginia. Virginia Law Review Charlottesville, VA, 58 : 97, January 1972.
Capstick, W.P. *Capital theft and the Cameroon Penal Code Amendment Ordinance, 1972.* British Journal of Criminology. London, 13 : 282-286, July 1973.
Carlson and Kenson : *In support of capital punishment.* On the Line. College Park, MD, 7 : 2, 1984, no. 1.
Carpentier, E.F. *The Christian context. In* The hanging question. Edited by L. Blom-Cooper. London, Duckworth and Co., 1969, p. 29-38.
Caron, P.L. *The capital defendant's right to obtain exculpatory evidence*

from the prosecution to present in mitigation before sentencing. American Criminal Law Review. Chicago, IL, 23 : 207-242, Fall 1985.
Carranca y Rivas, R. *Enfoques sobre la pena de muerte (Spotlights on the death penalty).* Criminalia. México, D.F., 39 : 199-210, julio-agosto 1973.
Carrington, F.G. *Neither cruel nor unusual – The case for capital punishment.* New Rochelle, N.Y., Arlington House Publishers, 1978, 223 p.
Carroll, J.M. *Death penalty provision of the new penal code.* Kentucky Bar Journal. Frankfort, KY, 38 : 15-21, October 1974.
Carroll, O. *The shadow of the gallows.* Penal Reformer. London, 1, April 1935.
Carter, R.M. and LaMont Smith A. *The death penalty in California : a statistical and composite portrait.* Crime and Delinquency. Hackensack, N.J., 15 : 62-76, January 1969.
Carvajal Moreno, P. *La pena de muerte y los derechos humanos (The death penalty and human rights).* Policia Espanola. Madrid, 10 : 32-35, 1971.
The Case against hanging. Police Review. London, no. 4513 : 1134-1137, 1979.
Casey, D.A. Grigsby v. Marby : *A new look at death-qualified juries.* American Criminal Law Review. Chicago, IL, 18 : 145-163, 1980, no. 1.
Casscells, W. and W.J. Cirran. *Doctors, the death penalty, and lethal injections. Recent developments.* New England Journal of Medicine. Boston, MA, 307 : 1532-1533, 1982, no. 24.
Castro, I.M. *Sorteo de condenados a la pena capital (Ballot for those condemed to death).* Revista de Criminologia y Ciencias Penales (La Paz), no. 4 : 99-101, mayo 1974.
Caswell, S. *Capital punishment : cementing a fragile victory.* Trial. Washington, D.C., 10 : 47, May-June 1974.
Cate, C.L. ten. *Tot glorie der gerichtigheid. De geschiedenis van het brandmerken als lijfstraf in Nederland.* Amsterdam, 1975, 228 p.
Catholicus. *Pena di morte e chiesa cattolica : annotazioni critiche (The death penalty and the Catholic church : critical comments).* Roma, G. Volpe, 1981, 132 p.
Cattaneo, M.A. *La pena di morte tra morale e politica nel pensiero dell'illuminismo (The death penalty between morals and politics in the Age of Enlightenment).* Sociologia del Diritto. Milano, 10 : 7-34, 1983, no. 1.
Catz, R. *Federal habeas corpus and the death penalty : need for a preclusion doctrine.* University of California Davis Law Review. Davis, CA, 18 : 1077-1120, 1985.
Caudrey, A. *Save the children ?* New Society. London, 74 : 449-450, 1985, no. 1198.
Cederblom, J.B. and Munévar G. *The death penalty : the relevance of deterrence.* Criminal Justice Review. Atlanta, GA, 7 : 63-66, 1982, no. 1.
Chamblin, M.H. *Effect of sex on the imposition of the death penalty.* Paper presented at a symposium entitled « Extra-legal attributes affecting death penalty sentencing ». September 1979, New York, N.Y., 23 p.
Chambliss, W.J. *The deterrent influence of punishment.* Crime and Delinquency. Hackensack, N.J., 12 : 70-75, January 1966.
Chandler, D.B. *Capital punishment and the Canadian parliament : a test*

of Durkheim's hypothesis on repressive law. Ann. Arbor, MI, 1974, VII, 104 p.
Chandler, D.B. *Capital punishment in Canada. A sociological study of repressive law.* Toronto, Ont., McClelland and Stewart Ltd., 1976, 224 p.
Charpentier, J. and Naud A. Pour ou contre la peine de mort (Pros and cons of the death penalty). Paris, Berger-Levrault, 1967.
Chauncey, R. *Deterrence. Certainty, severity, and sky-jacking.* Criminology. Beverly Hills, CA, 12 : 447-473, 1975, no. 4.
Cheatwood, D. *Capital punishment and corrections : is there an impending crisis ?* Crime and Delinquency. Beverly Hills, CA, 31 : 461-480, 1985, no. 4.
Chessman, C. and Kunstler W.K. *Beyond a reasonable doubt ?* The original trial of Caryl Chessman. Westport, CN, Greenwood Press, 1973, 304 p.
Chipman, Jr. E.N. *Indiana death penalty – An exercise in constitutional futility.* Valparaiso University Law Review. Valparaiso, IN, 15 : 409-451, 1981, no. 2.
Chiricos, T. and Waldo G. *Punishment and crime : an examination of some empirical evidence.* Social Problems. South Bend, IN, 18 : 200-217, Fall 1970.
Chiu, H. *Capital punishment in mainland China : a study of some Yunnan Province documents.* Journal of Criminal Law and Criminology. Baltimore, MD, 68 : 374-398, 1977, no. 3.
Christianson, S. *Execution by lethal injection.* Criminal Law Bulletin. Boston, MA, 15 : 69-78, 1979, no. 1.
Christoph, J.B. *Capital punishment and British politics ; the British movement to abolish the death penalty, 1945-1957.* London, Allen and Unwin, 1962, 202 p.
Cic, M. *Teoreticke otazky cecoslovenskeho socialistickeho trestneho prava* (Theoretical problems of Czechoslovak socialist penal law). Bratislava, 1982.
Cieslak, M. *Problem kazy śmierci (The problem of the death penalty).* Państwo i Prawo. Warsaw, no. 12 : 833-853, 1966.
Clark, F.H. *The death penalty in Illinois. In* Proceeding of the Illinois State Bar Association. Springfield, IL, 1927, p. 173-181.
Clark, R. *The death penalty and reverence for life. In* Crime in America. By R. Clark, New York, N.Y., Simon and Schuster, 1970, 346 p.
Clark, R. *Spenkelink's last appeal. In* The death penalty Edited by H.A. Bedau, 3rd ed. Oxford. Oxford University Press, 1982, p. 224-233.
Clark, R. *Statement before the Subcommittee on Criminal Laws and Procedures of the Senate Judiciary Committee on S. 1760 to abolish the death penalty, 2 July 1968.* Washington, D.C., 1968.
Cloché, P. *Le conseil athénien des cinq cents et la peine de mort* (The Athenian Council of the Five Hundred and the death penalty). Revue des Etudes Grecques, Paris, 1920.
Cloninger, D. *Deterrence and the death penalty : a cross-sectional analysis.* Journal of Behavioural Economics. Macomb, IL, 6 : 87-101, 1977.
Cluff, J.D. *Footnote to Furman : failing justification for the capital case exception to the right to bail after abolition of the death penalty.* San Diego

Law Review. San Diego, CA, 10 : 349-379, February 1973.
Cobin, H.L. *Abolition and restoration of the death penalty in Delaware. In* The death penalty in America ; an anthology. Edited by H.A. Bedau. Garden City, N.Y., Anchor Books, 1964, p. 359-373.
Coester, E. *Terrorisme et peine de mort (Terrorism and the death penalty).* Revue Pénitentiaire et de Droit Pénal, Paris, 109 : 141-150, avril-juin 1985.
Cohen, B.L. *Law without order. Capital punishment and the liberals.* New Rochelle, N.Y., Arlington House, 1970.
Cohen, C. *Shall we go a hanging ?* Penal Reformer. London, 1, October, 1934.
Cohen, N.P. *Can they kill me if I'm gone : trial in absentia in capital cases.* University of Florida Law Review. Gainesville, FL, 36 : 273-287, 1984, no. 2.
Coleman, R. *Cheaper than the chair : a look at capital expenses.* Student Lawyer. Chicago, IL, 14 : 4-5, 1985.
Colin, M. *Sociopathologie de la peine de mort (The socio-pathology of capital punishment).* Bulletin de Médecine Légale et de Toxicologie Médicale, Lyon, 15 : 292-295, 1972, n° 5.
Collignon, T. *Faut-il supprimer la peine de mort ? (Should the death penalty be abolished ?)* Revue de Droit Pénal et de Criminologie, Bruxelles,334-360, 1947, 48.
Colquitt, J.A. *The death penalty laws of Alabama.* Alabama Law Review. University, AL, 33 : 213-351, 1982, no. 2.
Colussi, J.A. *The unconstitutionality of death qualifying a jury prior to the determination of guilt : the fair cross-section requirement in capital cases.* Creighton Law Review. Omaha, NE, 15 : 595-617, 1981-82, no. 3.
Combs, M.W. and Comer, J.C. *Race and capital punishment : a longitudinal analysis.* Phylon. Atlanta, GA, 43 : 350-359, 1982, no. 4.
Combs, M.W. *The Supreme Court and capital punishment : uncertainty, ambiguity, and judicial control.* Southern University Law Review. Baton Rouge, LA, 7 : 1-41, 1980, no. 1.
The Committee on Civil Rights. The death penalty. Record of the Association of the Bar of the City of New York. New York, N.Y., 39 : 419-435, 1984, no. 5.
Comparison of the executed and the commuted among admissions to death row. By M.E. Wolfgang and others. Journal of Criminal Law, Criminology and Police Science. Baltimore, MD, 53 : 301-311, September 1962.
Conference on the Abolition of the Death Penalty, Stockholm, 10-11 December 1977. Report, London, Amnesty International Publications, 1977, 35 p.
Congressional rebirth of the death penalty : guiding the jury past Furman v. Georgia. Northwest University Law Review. Chicago, IL, 68 : 893-907, 1973, no. 5.
Conners, C.S. *The death penalty in military courts : constitutionally imposed ?* University of California – Los Angeles Law Review. Los Angeles, CA, 30 : 366-404, 1982, no. 2.
Conrad, J.P. *Research and development in corrections.* Federal Probation. Washington, D.C., 48 : 59-62, 1984, no. 2.
Constant, J. *De l'application de la peine de mort en matière d'assassinat*

(On the application of the death penalty for murder). Revue Pénitentiaire et de Droit Pénal, Paris, 75 : 893-907, 1951.
Constant, J. *Voltaire et la réforme des lois pénales (Voltaire and the reform of criminal law).* Revue de Droit Pénal et de Criminologie, Bruxelles, 537, 1958-1959.
Constitutionality of the Connecticut penal code (title 53a) guilty plea/capital punishment provisions. Connecticut Bar Journal. Hartfort, CT : 45, 1971.
Constitutionality of the death penalty for non-aggravated rape. Washington University Law Quarterly. St. Louis, MO : 170, Winter, 1972.
Contre ou pour la peine de mort. Etude de l'Institut de Criminologie de Paris, sous la direction de Jacques Léauté (Against and for the death penalty. Study by the Criminological Institute of Paris directed by Jacques Léauté). Librairie philosophique J. Vrin, Paris, 1979, 176 p.
Conway, D. *Capital punishment and deterrence : some consideration in dialogue form.* Philosophy and Public Affairs. Princeton, N.J., 3 : 431-443, 1974, no. 4.
Coody, D.W. *Fifth and sixth amendments – Privilege against self incrimination and right to counsel – Compelled competency examinations in capital punishment cases.* Estelle v. Smith. 101 S. Ct. 1866 (1981). American Journal of Criminal Law. Austin, TX, 10 : 65-78, 1982, no. 1.
Cook, E.H. Death penalty since Witherspoon and Furman. Monticello, IL, Vance Bibliographies, 1979, 28 p.
Coon, T.F. On crime and punishment... and the death penalty. Tennessee Law Enforcement Journal. Chattanooga, TN, 25 : 17-19, 1981, no. 4.
Copper, D.D. *Lesson of the scaffold : the public execution controversy in Victorian England.* Athens, OH, Ohio University Press, 1974, 212 p.
Cooper, R. *Capital punishment : helplessness and power.* Encounter. Milton, ON, 46 : 163-175, Spring 1985.
Corbetta, P. and Parisi A. *L'opinione pubblica italiana di fronte alla pena di morte (Italian public opinion regarding the death penalty). In* La pena di morte nel mondo. By Amnesty International. Casale Monferrato, Marietti, 1983, p. 33.
Cornil, P. *La peine de mort, sanction anachronique ; notes de politique criminelle et de philosophie pénale (The death penalty, anachronistic punishment : notes on criminal policy and penal philosophy). In* Epistemonike epeteris. Etudes en l'honneur de D.I. Karanikas. Thessalonika, 1966, p. 569-586.
Corre, A. *A propos de la peine de mort (On the death penalty).* Archives d'Anthropologie Criminelle et de Criminologie, Paris, 15 mars 1908.
Correia, E. *La peine de mort (The death penalty). In* Pena de morte. Colòquio Internacional Comemorativo do Centenario da Abolicao da Pena de Morte em Portugal. Vol. 1 Coimbra, Faculdade de Direito da Universidade de Coimbra, 1967, p. 23-37.
Council of Europe. *Conference of European Ministers of Justice,* 12th, Luxembourg, 20-21 May 1980. *The death penalty.* Strasbourg, 1980. MJU-12 (80) 5. 8 p.
Council of Europe. *European Committee on Crime Problems.* Abolition of the death penalty. Strasbourg, 1979, 10 p.

Council of Europe. *Common opinion regarding the death penalty* – Decision CM/210/311080. Strasbourg, 1981. 3 p. CDPC (81) 13 Add. VI.
Council of Europe. *The death penalty.* Strasbourg, 1980. 18 p. CDPC (80) 23.
Council of Europe. *Human Rights. Abolition de la peine de mort en Europe.* Strasbourg, 1983. 3 p. B (83) 2.
Council of Europe. *Protocol No. 6 to the Convention for the Protection of Human Rights and Fundamental Freedoms concerning the Abolition of the Death Penalty.* Strasbourg, 1983, 7 p. H (83) 3.
Cowan, C.L., Thompson, W.C. and Ellsworth, P.C. *The effects of death qualification on jurors' predisposition to convict and on the quality of deliberation.* Law and Human Behavior. New York, N.Y., 8 : 53-79, 1984, no. 1/2.
Cross, R. *Some secondary arguments. In* The hanging question. Edited by L. Blom-Cooper. London, Duckworth and Co., 1969, p. 43-54.
Crowns, A.J. Jr. *Death penalty – A national dilemma. In* Critical issues in criminal justice. By R.G. Iacovetta and D.H. Chang. Durnam, N.C., Carolina Academic Press, 1979.
The Cruel and unusual punishment clause and the substantive criminal law. Harvard Law Review. Cambridge, MA, 79 : 635-655, January 1966.
Crut, D. *La peine de mort a-t-elle sa raison d'être ? (Is there any reason for the death penalty to exist ?)* Vie Judiciaire, Paris : 1, 6-7, 8-14 December 1969.
Cuello Calon, E. *Contribución al estudio de la historia de la pena de muerte en Espana (Contribution to the study of the history of the death penalty in Spain).* Anuario de Derecho Penal y Ciencias Penales. Madrid, 10 : 9-39, enero-abril 1957.
Culver, J.H. *The states and capital punishment : executions from 1977-1984.* Justice Quarterly. Lincoln, NE, 2 : 567-578, 1985, no. 4.
Cunningham, C. *Some practical considerations. In* The hanging question. Edited by L. Blom-Cooper. London, Duckworth and Co., 1969, p. 109-114.
Curran, W.J. and Casscells, W. *The ethics of medical participation in capital punishment by intravenous drug injection.* New England Journal of Medicine. Boston, MA, 302 : 226-230, January 1980.
Curran, W.J. *Psychiatric evaluations and mitigating circumstances in capital punishment sentencing.* New England Journal of Medicine, Boston, MA, 307 : 1431-1432, 1982, no. 23.
Curran, W.J. *Uncertainty in prognosis of violent conduct : the Supreme Court lays down the law.* New England Journal of Medicine, Boston, MA, 310 : 1651-1652, 1984.
Current comment. Penal Reformer. London, 3, October 1936.
Cutler, E.J. *Capital punishment and lynching.* Annals of the American Academy of Political and Social Science. Philadelphia, PA, 29 : 622-625, 1907.
Cutler, S. *Criminal punishment – Legal and moral considerations.* Catholic Lawyer. Jamaica, N.Y., 6 : 110-125, Spring 1960.
Dahlstrom, W.G. *Utility of the Megargee-Bohn MMPI typological assignments : study with a sample of death row inmates.* Criminal Justice and Behavior. Beverly Hills, CA, 13 : 5-17, 1986, no. 1.

Daiches, D. *A primitive sanction. In* The hanging question. Edited by L. Blom-Cooper. London, Duckworth and Co., 1969, 138 p.
Dake, N. *Who deservs to live – who deservs to die : reflections on capital punishment.* Currents in Theology and Mission. St. Louis, MO, 10 : 67-77, April 1983.
Damour, L. *La confusion des peines capitales et l'influence des mesures de grâce sur l'exécution de ces peines (The confusion of death penalties and the influence of pardon on their application).* Revue de Sciences Criminelle et de Droit Pénal Comparé, Paris, 577-563, 1957.
Daniels, S. *Social science and death penalty cases.* Law and Policy Quarterly. Beverly Hills, CA, 336-372, July 1979.
Dann, R.H. *Abolition and restoration of the death penalty in Oregon. In* The death penalty in America ; an anthology. Edited by H.A. Bedau, Harden City, N.Y. Anchor Books, 1964, p. 343-351.
Dann, R.H. *Capital punishment in Oregon.* Annals of the American Academy of Political and Social Science. Philadelphia, PA : 110-115, November 1952.
Dann, R.H. *The deterrent effect of capital punishment.* Philadelphia, PA, The Committee of Philantropic Labor of Philadelphia Yearly Meeting of Friends, 1935.
Danto, B.L. *Alternative approaches to the violent criminal.* International Journal of Offender Therapy and Comparative Criminology. London, 23 : 11-20, 1979, no. 1.
Dareste, R. *Esquisse du droit criminel athénien (A sketch of Athenian criminal law).* Journal des Savants, Paris, 1878.
Darrow, C. *The futility of the death penalty. In* Verdicts out of court. Edited by A. Weinberg. Chicago, Quadrangle, 1963.
Darrow, C. *Is capital punishment a wise policy ? In* Attorney for the damned. Edited by A. Weinberg. New York, N.Y., Simon and Schuster, 1957, p. 89-103.
Darrow, C. *Why capital punishment ? In* The story of my life. By C. Darrow. New York, N.Y., C. Scribner's Sons, 1932, p. 359-375.
Davies, C. *Permissive Britain : social change in the sixties and seventies.* London, Pitman Publishing, 1975, 246 p.
Davis, C. *Waiting for it.* New York, N.Y., 1980, X, 182 p.
Davis, D.B. *Movement to abolish capital punishment in America, 1787-1861.* American Historical Review. Richmond, VA, 63 : 23-46, October 1957.
Davis, M. *Death, deterrence, and the method of common sense.* Social Theory and Practice. Tallahassee, FL, no. 772 : 145-177, 1981.
Davis, M. *Is the death penalty irrevocable ?* Social Theory and Practice. Tallahassee, FL, 10 : 143-156, 1984, no. 2.
Davis, P.C. *The death penalty and the current state of the law.* Criminal Law Bulletin. Boston, MA, 14 : 7-17, 1978, no. 1.
Davis, P.C. *Texas capital sentencing procedures : the role of the jury and the restraining hand of the expert.* Journal of Criminal Law and Criminology. Chicago, IL, 69 : 300-310, 1978, no. 3.
Davis, R.A. *Capital punishment and the Pennsylvania Prison Society.* Prison Journal. Philadelphia, PA, 53 : 72-74, Spring-Summer 1973.

Davis, R.P. *Tasmanian gallows : a study of capital punishment.* Hobart, Cat and Fiddle, 1974, XV, 119 p.
Dawtry, F. *The abolition of the death penalty in Britain.* British Journal of Criminology. London, 6 : 183-192, 1966.
Dayan, M. *Payment of costs in death penalty cases.* Criminal Law Bulletin. Boston, MA, 22 : 18-28, 1986, no. 1.
De Lalla, A. *La pena di morte nell'esame delle organizzazioni internazionali di studi giuridici (The death penalty as seem by international organizations of legal studies).* Archivio Penale. Roma, 19 : 464-469, novembre-dicembre 1963.
De Landecho, C.M. *Reflexion criminologica sobre la pena de muerte (Crimonological reflections on the death penalty).* Razon y Fe. Madrid : 22, diciembre 1970.
De Merich, G. *Va in pensione la « pietosa assassina » (The « merciful murderer » retires).* Polizia Moderna. Roma, 33 : 24-28, 1981, no. 11.
De Wolfe, T. and Jackson L.A. *Birds of a brighter feather : leval of moral reasoning and similarity of attitude as determinants of interpersonal attraction.* Psychological Reports. Missoula, MT, 54 : 303-308, 1984, no. 1
Death – California style : reviewing the constitutionality of the State's new capital punishment law. University of San Fernando Valley Law Review. Sepulveda, CA, 3 : 145-157, 1974.
Death as a penalty for rape is cruel and unusual punishment. Wisconsin Law Review. Madison, WI, no. 1 : 253-268, 1978.
Death penalty. Bulletin of the Canadian Criminology and Corrections Association. Ottawa, Ont., 2 : 1 and 3, January 1973.
Death penalty. Correctional Process. Ottawa, Ont., 10 : 3, September 1969.
Death penalty. Crime and delinquency. Hackensack, N.Y., 19 : 577-578, October 1973, no. 4.
The Death penalty. Penal Reform News/Strafhervormingsnuus. Pretoria, 57 : 18-20, January 1962.
Death penalty again. Bulletin of the Canadian Criminology and Corrections Association. Ottawa, Ont., 2 : 1 and 3, September 1972.
The Death penalty and abortion. In Letter to the President on crime control, By N. Morris and G. Hawkins. Chicago, IL, University of Chicago Press, 1977, 96 p.
Death penalty in Massachusetts. Suffolk University Law Review. Boston, MA, 8 : 632-681, Spring 1974.
The Death penalty in South Africa. London, Amnesty International Publications, 1980.
The Death penalty in Victoria (editorial). Australian and New Zealand Journal of Criminology. Melbourne, 9 : 5-6, March 1976.
Death penalty is not cruel within the meaning of the Canadian Bill of Rights. Bulletin of the Canadian Criminology and Corrections Association. Ottawa, Ont., 6 : 3, January 1977.
Death penalty : shortening the journey from death sentence to execution : eliminating procedural safeguards ; reliability of psychiatric evidence. Ann. Surv. Am., 1984.
The Death-qualified jury and the defense of insanity. Law and Human Behavior. New York, N.Y., 8 : 81-93, 1984, no. 1/2.

Death row conditions : progression toward constitutional protections. Akron Law Review. Akron, OH, 19 : 293-310, 1985.

Decker, S.H. and Kohfeld, C.W. *A deterrence study of the death penalty in Illinois, 1933-1980.* Journal of Criminal Justice. New York, N.Y., 12 : 367-378, 1984, no. 4.

Decourrière, A. *L'abolition de la peine de mort en France (The abolition of the death penalty in France).* Revue de Droit Pénal et de Criminologie. Bruxelles, 62 : 485-489, 1982.

Del Rosal, J. *Cuatro pena de muerte, cuatro, (Four death penalties, four),* vo. I. Madrid, Instituto de Criminologia, Universidad complutense de Madrid, 1973, 260 p.

Del Rosal, J. *Cuatro penas de muerte, cuatro,* vol. II. Madrid, Instituto de Criminologia, Universidad Complutense de Madrid, 1973, 260 p.

DeMarcus, J.P. *Capital punishment.* Frankfort, KY, Kentucky Legislative Research Commission, 1965. Information Bulletin, no. 40.

Demierre, E. *Le problème de la peine de mort en Grande-Bretagne (The problem of the death penalty in Great Britain).* Revue Internationale de Criminologie et de Police Technique, Genève, 19 : 39-47, janvier-mars 1965.

Destrée, A. *Opium et peine de mort en Iran (Optium and the death penalty in Iran).* Revue de Droit Pénal et de Criminologie, Bruxelles, 52 : 568-589, février 1972.

Deterrence and the death penalty : a temporal cross-sectional approach. Journal of Criminal Law and Criminology. Baltimore, MD, 70 : 235-254, 1979, no. 2.

DeVries, B. and Walker, S.J. *Moral reasoning and attitudes toward capital punishment.* Developmental Psychology. Washington, D.C., 22 : 509-513, 1986, no. 4.

Diamond, B.L. *Murder and the death penalty : a case report.* American Journal of Orthopsychiatry. Albany, N.Y., 45 : 712-722, 1975, no. 4. Also in Capital punishment in the United States. Edited by H.A. Bedau and C.M. Pierce, New York, N.Y., AMS Press, 1976, p. 445-460.

Dike, S.T. *Capital punishment in the United States : a consideration of the evidence.* Hackensack, N.J., National Council on Crime and Delinquency, 1982, 101 p.

Dike, S.T. *Capital punishment in the United States. Part I : Observations on the use and interpretation of the law.* Criminal Justice Abstracts. Hackensack, N.J., 13 : 283-311, 1981, no. 2. *Part II : Empirical evidence.* Criminal Justice Abstracts. Hackensack, N.J., 13 : 426-447, 1981, no. 3. *Part III : The Practice – actual and proposed.* Criminal Justice Abstracts. Hackensack, N.J., 13 : 577-597, 1981, no. 4.

Dikijian, A. *Capital punishment : a selected bibliography, 1940-1968.* Crime and Delinquency. Hackensack, N.J., 15 : 162-164, 1969, no. 1.

Dinamar Misael, D. *A pena de morte face a os delitos atentatórios à sugurança nacional (The death penalty regarding crimes against national security).* Revista da Policia Civil. Curitiba, 2 : 29-35, julio-dicembre 1971.

DiSalle, M.V. *Comments on capital punishment and clemency.* Ohio State Law Journal. Columbus, OH, 25 : 71-77, 1964.

DiSalle, M.V. *Justice, the law and capital punishment.* American Journal of Psychiatry. Washington, D.C., 123 : 1359-1360, 1967, no. 11.

DiSalle, M.V. and Blochman, L.G. *The power of life or death.* New York, N.Y., Random House, 1965.
DiSalle, M.V. *Special message on capital punishment.* Senate Journal. Columbus, OH : 5-13, 10 February 1959.
DiSalle, M.V. *Trends in the abolition of capiunishment.* University of Toledo Law Review. Toledo, OH, 1 : 1-13, Winter 1969.
Discretion and the constitutionality of the new death penalty statutes. Harvard Law Review. Cambridge, MA, 87 : 1690-1719, 1974, no. 8.
Disparities in sentencing. In The growth of crime. By L. Radzinowicz and J. King. New York, N.Y., Basic Books Inc., 1977, p. 206-212.
Distinguishing among murders : assessing the proportionality of the death penalty. Columbia Law Review. New York, N.Y., 85 : 1788-1807, 1985.
Dix, G.E. *Administration of the Texas death penalty statutes : constitutional infirmities related to the prediction of dangerousness.* Texas Law Review. Austin, TX, 55 : 1343-1414, 1977, no. 8.
Dix, G.E. *Appellate review of the decision to impose death.* Georgetown Law Journal. Washington, D.C., 68 : 97-161, 1979, no. 1.
Dix, G.E. *The death penalty, " dangerousness ", psychiatric testimony and professional ethics.* American Journal of Criminal Law. Austin, TX, 5 : 151-214, 1977, no. 2.
Dix, G.E. *Expert prediction testimony in capital sentencing : evidentiary and constitutional consideration.* American Criminal Law Review. Chicago, IL, 19 : 1-48, 1981, no. 1.
Dix, G.E. *Participation by mental health professionals in capital murder sentencing.* International Journal of Law and Psychiatry. Elmsford, N.Y., 1 : 283-308, 1978.
Dix, G.E. *Psychological abnormality and capital sentencing. The new " diminished responsibility ".* International Journal of Law and Psychiatry. Elmsford, N.Y., 7 : 249-267, 1984, no. 3.
Doleschal, E. *The deterrent effect of legal punishment.* Information Review on Crime and Delinquency. New York, N.Y., 1 : 1-17, 1969, no. 7.
Domozick, D.D. *Fact or fiction : mitigating the death penalty in Ohio.* Cleveland State Law Review. Cleveland, OH, 32 : 263-293, 1983-84, no. 2.
Donnedieu de Vabres, H. *La politique criminelle des états autoritaires (Criminal policy in authoritarian states).* Paris, Sirey, 1938.
Donnell, H.E. *To hang by the neck.* Prison World. Boston, MA, 4 : 6-8 and 31, July-August 1942.
Donnelly, R.C. and Brewster, C.W. *Capital punishment in Connecticut.* Connecticut Bar journal. Rocky Hill, CT, 35 : 39-56, 1961.
Donnelly, S.J.M. *A theory of justice, judicial methodology, and the constitutionality of capital punishment : Rawls, Dworkin, and a theory of criminal responsability.* Syracuse Law Review. Syracuse, N.Y., 29 : 1109-1174, 1978, no. 4.
Dorin, D.D. *Two different worlds : criminologists, justices and racial discrimination in the imposition of capital punishment in rape cases.* Journal of Criminal Law and Criminology. Chicago, IL, 72 : 1667-1698, 1981, no. 4.
Douglas, C. *The death penalty : Chinese style.* Trial. Washington, D.C., 13 : 44-46, 1977, no. 2.

Drabble, M. *A corrupting influence. In* The hanging question. Edited by L. Blom-Cooper. London, Duckworth and Co., 1969, p. 55-62.
Drahozal, C.R. *Wainwright v. Witt and death qualified juries : a changed standard but an unchanged result.* Iowa Law Review. Iowa City, IA, 71 : 1187-1208, 1986, no. 4.
Draper, Th. ed., *Capital punishment.* New York, N.Y., H.W. Wilson, 1985, 166 p.
Dressler, D. *Capital punishment is murder !* Coronet. New York, N.Y., 47 : 135-140, January 1960.
Dressler, J. *The jurisprudence of death by another : accessories and capital punishment.* University of Colorado Law Review. Boulder, CO, 51 : 17-75, 1979, no. 1.
Drzazga, J. *Capital punishment.* Law and Order. New York, N.Y., 9 : 88-89. December 1961.
Duff, C. *A handbook on hanging.* London, Putnam, 1974.
Duff, C. *A new handbook on hanging.* Chicago, IL, Henry Regnery Co., 1955. London, Hamilton and Co., 1956, 192 p.
Duffy, C.T. and Hirschberg, A. *Eighty-eight men and two women.* Garden City, N.Y., Doubleday, 1962.
Dugard, J. *Death penalty in South Africa. In* Human rights and the South African legal order. By J. Dugard. Princeton, N.J., Princeton University Press, 1971.
Dunlavey, M.A. *Is capital punishment worth keeping ?* Law and Order. New York, N.Y., 20 : 92-96, 1972, no. 6.
Duparc, P. *Origines de la grâce dans le droit pénal romain et français... (Origins of pardon in Roman and French criminal law...).* Paris, Sirey, 1942.
Dupreel, J. *Lombroso et la pénologie (Lombroso and penology).* Revue de Science Criminelle et de droit Pénal Comparé, Paris, no. 3 : 535-540, 1977.
Edison, M. *The empirical assault on capital punishment.* Journal of Legal Education. Lexington, KY, 23 : 2-15, 1971.
Edwards, J.Ll.J. The Homicide Act 1957 : a critique. British Journal of Delinquency. London : 8, July 1957.
Edwards, S.W. *The death penalty.* State Bar Journal of California. San Francisco, CA, 25 : 98-101, January-February 1950.
Ehrhardt, C.W. and Levinson, L.H. *The aftermath of Furman : the Florida experience. I. The future of capital punishment in Florida : analysis and recomendations. II. Florida's legislative response to Furman : an exercice in futility ?* Journal of Criminal Law and Criminology. Baltimore, MD, 64 : 2-21, March 1973.
Ehrenzweig, A.A. *A psychoanalysis of the insanity plea : clues to the problems of criminal responsability and insanity in the death cell.* Criminal Law Bulletin. Boston, MA, 1 : 3, 1965.
Ehrlich, I. *Capital punishment and deterrence – Some further thoughts and additional evidence. In* Criminology review yearbook. vol. 1. Edited by S.L. Messinger and E. Bittner. Beverly Hills, CA, Sage, 1979, p. 142-189.
Ehrlich, I. *Deterrence : evidence and inference.* Yale Law Journal. New Haven, CT, 85 : 209-226, December 1975.
Ehrlich, I. *The deterrent effect of capital punishment : a question of life*

and death. American Economic Review. Providence, R.I., 65 : 397-417, June 1975.
Ehrlich, I. *Fear of deterrence. A critical evaluation of the Report of the Panel on Research on Deterrent and Incapacitative Effects.* Journal of Legal Studies. Chicago, IL, 6 : 293-316, 1977, no. 2.
Ehrlich, I. and Gibbons, J.C. *On the measurement of the deterrent effect of capital punishment and the theory of deterrence.* Journal of Legal Studies. Chicago, IL, 6 : 35-50, 1977, no. 1.
Ehrmann, H.B. *The case that will not die :* Commonwealth v. Sacco and Vanzetti. Boston, MA, Little, Brown and Co., 1969, 576 p.
Ehrmann, H.B. *The death penalty and the administration of justice.* Annals of the American Academy of Political and Social Science. Philadelphia, PA, no. 284 : 73-84, November 1952.
Ehrmann, S.R. *American League looks at capital punishment. In* Proceedings of the 86th Annual Congress of Correction. Washington, D.C., American Correctional Association, 1956, p. 300-308.
Ehrmann, S.R. *For whom the chair waits.* Federal Probation. Washington, D.C., 26 : 14-25, March 1962.
Ehrmann, S.R. *The human side of capital punishment. In* The death penalty in America ; an anthology. Edited by H.A. Bedau. Garden City, N.Y., Anchor Books, 1964, p. 492-519.
Eighth amendment – *The death penalty and vicarious felony murder : nontriggerman may not be executed absent a finding of an intent to kill,* Enmund v. Florida. 102 S. Ct. 3368 (1982). Journal of Criminal Law and Criminology. Chicago, IL, 73 : 1553-1571, 1982, no. 4.
Eighth amendment – *Minors and the death penalty : decision and avoidance,* Eddings v. Oklahoma. 102 S. Ct. 869 (1982). Journal of Criminal Law and Criminology. Chicago, IL, 73 : 1525-1552, 1982, no. 4.
Eighth amendment – *Proportionality review of death sentences not required.* Journal of Criminal Law and Criminology. Chicago, IL, 75 : 839-854, 1984.
Eighth amendment – *Trial court may impose death sentence despite jury's recommandation of life.* Journal of Criminal Law and Criminology. Chicago, IL, 75 : 813-828, 1984.
Elliot, R. *Agent of death : the memories of an executioner.* New York, N.Y., Dutton, 1940.
Ellis, H.D. *Constitutional law : the death penalty : a critique of the philosophical bases held to satisfy the eighth amendment requirements for its justification.* Oklahoma Law Review. Norman, OK, 34 : 567-613, 1981, no. 3.
Elliston, F.A. *Deadly force : an ethical analysis.* Paper presented at a conference on police ethics 22-25 April 1982. New York, N.Y., John Jay College of Criminal Justice, 1982, 22 p.
Elliston, F.A. *Deadly force and capital punishment. In* Police ethics ; hard choices in law enforcement. Edited by W.C. Heffernan and T. Stroup. New York, N.Y., John Jay Press, 1985, p. 153-167.
Ellsworth, P.C. *Empirical data and judicial decisions : examples from capital punishment research.* Paper presented at the American Psychological Association Convention. Chicago, IL, 1 September 1975.

Ellsworth, P.C. *Juries on trial.* Psychology Today. New York, N.Y., 19 : 44-46, 1985, no. 7.

Ellsworth, P.C. and Ross, L. *Public opinion and capital punishment : a close examination of the view of abolitionists and retentionists.* Crime and Delinquency. San Francisco, CA, 29 : 116-169, 1983, no. 1

Ellsworth, P.C. and Ross, L. *Public opinion and judicial decision making : an example from research on capital punishment. In* Capital punishment in the United States. Edited by H.A. Bedau and C.M. Pierce. New York, N.Y., AMS Press, 1976, p. 152-171.

Endres, M.E. *The morality of capital punishment : equal justice under the law ?* Mystic, CT, Twenty-Third Publications, 1985.

Engel, P.F. *The abolition of capital punishment in New Zealand,* 1935-1961. Wellington, 1977.

England, J.C. *Capital punishment in the light of constitutional evolution – An analysis of distinctions between Furman and Gregg.* Notre Dame Lawyer. Notre Dame, IN, 52 : 596-610, 1977, no. 4.

England, L.R. *Capital punishment and open-end questions.* Public Opinion Quarterly. New York, N.Y., 12 : 412-416, 1948.

Enrique, C.H. *Ojeada sobre psicologia profunda de la pena de muerte (A glance at the deep psychology of capital punishment).* Criminalistica (Havana) : 28-39, marzo-abril 1955.

Erez, E. *Thou shalt not execute : the attitude of Hebrew law toward capital punishment.* Paper presented at the Interdisciplinary Conference on Capital Punishment, April 1980. Atlanta, GA, Georgia State University.

Erickson, M. and Gibbs, J. *The deterrence question : some alternative methods of analysis.* Social Science Quarterly. Austin, TX, no. 54 : 534-551, December 1973.

Erskine, H. *The polls : capital punishment.* Public Opinion Quarterly. New York, N.Y., 34 : 290-307, 1970.

Escaich, R. *Cet éternel problème : maintien ou suppression de la peine de mort (The perennial problem : maintain or abolish the death penalty).* Revue Internationale de Criminologie et de Police Technique, Genève, 31 : 119-122, 1978, no. 2.

Eshelman, B.E. and Riley F. *Death row chaplain. Englewood Cliffs,* N.J., Prentice Hall, 1962, 252 p.

Espy, Jr. M.W. *Capital punishment and deterrence : what the statistics cannot show.* Crime and delinquency. Hackensack, N.J., 26 : 537-544, 1980, no. 4.

Espy, Jr. M.W. *The Historical perspective. In* Slow coming dark. By D. Magee. New York, N.Y., Pilgrim Press, 1980, p. 163-174.

Eugster, J. *La peine de mort dans le droit pénal militaire suisse (The death penalty in Swiss military criminal law).* Revue Internationale de Criminologie et Police Technique, Genève, 6 : 293-299, octobre-décembre 1961.

Evolution de la législation sur la peine capitale en Europe (The evolution of European legislation on capital punishment). Revue de Science Criminelle et de Droit Pénal Comparé, Paris, n° 2 : 411-415, 1979.

Ewing, C.P. Dr. « *Death* » *and the case for an ethical ban on psychiatric and psychological predictions of dangerousness in capital sentencing pro-*

ceedings. American Journal of Law and Medicine. Boston, MA, 8 : 408-428, 1983.

Ewing, C.P. Dr. *Psychologists and psychiatrists in capital sentencing : experts or executioners ?* Social Action and the Law. Brooklyn, N.Y., 8 : 67, 1982.

L'Execution capitale par asphyxie (Death by asphyxiation). Revue de Droit Pénal et de Criminologie, Bruxelles : 308, 1922.

Executions in U.S.A. – Seven so far this year and many more expected. Amnesty International Newsletter. London, 14 : 1-3, 1984, no. 5.

The Executioner's song : is there a right to listen ! Virginia Law Review. Charlottesville, VA, 69 : 374-403, 1983, no. 2.

Executive clemency in capital cases. New York University Law Review. New York, N.Y., 39 : 136-192, January 1967.

L'exil comme substitut à la peine de mort (Exile as an alternative to capital punishment). Revue de Science Criminelle et de Droit Pénal Comparé, Paris, n° 4 : 963-964, 1979.

Faggan, R.W. *Police attitudes towards capital punishment.* Journal of Police Science and Administration. Gaithersburg, MD, 14 : 193-201, 1986, no. 3.

Faia, M.A. *Willful, deliberate, premeditated and irrational : reflections on the futility of executions.* State Government. Lexington, KY, 55 : 14-21, 1982, no. 1.

Fanning, C.E. *Ed. Selected articles on capital punishment.* Minneapolis, M.N., Wilson H.W., Co., 1913.

Fattah, E.A. *Canada's successful experience with the abolition of the death penalty.* Canadian Journal of Criminology. Ottawa, Ont., 25 : 421-431, 1983, no. 4.

Fattah, E.A. *The Canadian public and the death penalty ; a study of a social attitude.* Ottawa, Ont., Research and Systems Development Branch, Ministry of the Solicitor General, 1976.

Fattah, E.A. *Empirical studies of general deterrence : capital punishment research.* Canadian Journal of Criminology and Corrections, Ottawa, Ont. 19 : 33-38, April 1977.

Fattah, E.A. *Is capital punishment a unique deterrent ?* A dispassionate review of old and new evidence. Canadian Journal of Criminology, Ottawa, Ont., 23 : 291-311, 1981, no. 3.

Fattah, E.A. *Perceptions of violence, concern about crime, fear of victimization and attitudes to the death penalty.* Canadian Journal of Criminology, Ottawa, Ont., 21 : 22-38, 1979, no. 1.

Fattah, E.A. *The preventive mechanisms of the death penalty : a discussion.* Paper presented at the annual meeting of Academy of Criminal Justice Sciences, Chicago, IL, 27-30 March 1984. Crimcare Journal, 1 : 109-137, 1985, no. 2.

Fattah, E.A. *Sentencing to death – The inherent problem.* In New directions in sentencing. By Grosman B.A. Scarborough, Ont., Butterworths, 1980, p. 157-193.

Fattah, E.A. *A study of the deterrent effect of capital punishment with special reference to the Canadian situation.* Ottawa, Ont., Information Canada, 1972, 212 p.

Feldman, H. *Learning under penalty of death.* Prison Journal, Philadelphia, PA, 53 : 36-45, Autumn-Winter 1973.
Fernandes, R. *Pena de morte em Portugal.* The death penalty in Portugal. Revista da Ordem dos Advogados Lisboa, 31 : 5, janeiro-junio 1971.
Feucht, D. Grube und Pfahl. *Ein Beitrag zur Geschichte der deutschen Hinrichtungsbraeuche.* The cavity and the file. A contribution to the history of German execution procedures). Tuebingen, J.C.B. Mohr, 1967, 223 p.
Fiji – *Death sentence for murder – Discretion of tiral judge to certify proper case for not imposing death sentence.* Criminal Law Review, London, 202, March 1976.
Filler, L. *Movements to abolish the death penalty in the United States.* Annals of the American Academy of Political and Social Science, Philadelphia, PA, 284 : 124-136, November 1952.
Filota, F. *Protiv smrtne kazne.* Against capital punishment. Beograd, 1981.
Finch, M. and Ferraro M. *The empirical challenge to death-qualified juries : on further examination.* Nebraska Law Review, Lincoln, NE, 65 : 21-74, 1986.
Finding the death penalty cruel and unusual. University of Missouri-Kansas City Law Review, Kansas City, MO, 43 : 162-178, Winter 1974.
Finkel, R. *A survey of capital offenses.* In Capital punishment. Edited by T. Sellin. New York, N.Y., Harper and Row, 1967, p. 22-31.
Fisk, T. *A student's view.* In the hanging question. Edited by L. Blom-Cooper. London, Duckworth and Co., 1969, p. 73-82.
Fitzgerald, R. and Ellsworth P.C. *Due process vs. crime control.* Death qualification and jury attitudes. Law and Human Behavior, New York, NY, 8 : 35-51, 1984, no. 1/2.
Five-to-four vote kills capital punishment... almost. American Bar Association Journal, Chicago, IL 58 : 972-973, September 1972.
Florida Civil Liberties Union. Rape : selective electrocution based on race. Miami, FL, Florida Civil Liberties Union, 1964.
Florida death penalty : a lack of discretion ? University of Miami Law Review (Coral Gables, FL) 28 : 723-728, Spring 1974.
Florida's legislative and judicial responses to Furman v. Georgia : an analysis and criticism. Florida State University Law Review, Tallahassee, FL, 2 : 108-152, Winter 1974.
Foley, L.A. and Powell R. *The discretion of prosecutors, judges and juries in capital cases.* Criminal Justice Review Atlanta, GA, 7 : 10-22, 1982.
Foley, L.A. *Effect of race on the imposition of the death penalty.* Paper presented at a symposium entitled « Extra-legal attributes affecting death penalty sentencing », September 1979. New York, N.Y., 20 p.
Footnote to Furman : *failing justification for the capital case exception to the right to bail after abolition of the death penalty.* San Diego Law Review, San Diego, CA, 10 : 349, February 1973.
Forman, Jr. W.H. *De facto abolition of the death penalty in Louisiana.* Louisiana Bar Journal (New Orleans, LA) 18 : 199, December 1970.
Forst, B. *Capital punishment and deterrence : conflicting evidence ?* Journal of Criminal Law and Criminology, Chicago, IL, 74 : 927-942, 1983, no. 3.

Forst, B. *The deterrent effect of capital punishment : a cross-state analysis of the 1960's.* Minnesota Law Review, Minneapolis, MN, 61 : 743-767, May 1977, no. 5.

Fortenberry, J.H. *Socio-economic attributes affecting the imposition of the death penalty.* Paper presented at a symposium entitled « Extra-legal attributes affecting death penalty sentencing », September 1979. New York, N.Y. 24 p.

Fragoso, H.C. *Pena de morte.* The death penalty. Revista Brasileira de Criminologia e Direito Penal (Rio de Janeiro) 41-48, abril-junio, 1967.

France – *The abolition of capital punishment : the French experience.* Crime Prevention and Criminal Justice Newsletter (Vienna) no. 11 : 17-19, 1984.

France – *Comité d'Etudes sur la Violence, la Criminalité et la Délinquance.* Recommandation 103 : peine de mort. Study Committee on Violence, Criminality and Delinquency – Recommendation 103 – Capital punishment. In Réponses à la violence. Paris, La Documentation Française, 1977, p. 191-192.

Frank, J. and Frank, B. *Not guilty.* Garden City, NY, Doubleday, 1957.

Frankel, D.S. *The constitutionality of the mandatory death penalty for life-term prisoners who murder.* New York University Law Review, New York, NY, 55 : 636-670, 1980, no. 4.

Frankowski, S. *Dyskusja nad artykulem prof. M. Cislaka « Problem kary smierci ».* Discussion on the article by Prof. M. Cislaka « Problkems of the death penalty »). Panstwo i Prawo, Warsan no. 6, 1966.

Fraser, A. *G. ed. Capital punishment issue.* Prison Journal Philadelphia, PA, 12 : 1-28, October 1932.

Frede, L. *Die Todesstrafe bei Goethe.* The death penalty as seen by Goethe, 80 : 385-388, 1968, no. 2.

Freeman, I.H. *The making of a boy killer.* In the death penalty in America, an anthology. Edited by H.A. Bedau. Garden City, N.Y., Anchor Books, 1964, p. 548-556.

Freeman, M.D.A. *Retributivism and the death sentence. In Law, morality and rights.* Edited by M.A. Steward. Dordrecht, Reidel, 1983, p. 405-422.

French, L. *Blacks and capital punishment.* An assessment of latent discriminatory justice in the United States. Journal of Sociology and Social Welfare (West Hartford, CT) 6 : 231-244, 1979, no. 2.

Frez, F. *Thou shalt not execute.* Hebrew law perspective on capital punishment. Criminology (London) 19 : 25-43, 1981, no. 1.

Friedman, L. *The use of multiple regression analysis to test for a deterrent effect of capital punishment : prospects and problems.* Berkeley, CA, Graduate School of Business Administration, University of California, 1975. (Working paper no. 38).

Froidcourt, M. de. *La guillotine liégeoise.* The guillotine at Liege. Revue de Droit Pénal et de Criminologie (Bruxelles) : 77-89, 203-213 and 316-328, 1934.

Furman v. Georgia, *Deathknell for capital punishment ?* St. John's Law Review (Jamaïca, N.Y.), 47 : 107-147, October 1972.

Gabrielli, G. *La illecità della pena di morte (The death penalty is illegal).* Criminologia. Milano : 19-29, 1961.

Galbo, A. *Death after life : the future of New York's mandatory death penalty for murders committed by life-term prisoners.* Fordham Urban Law Journal. New York, N.Y., 13 : 567-638, 1984-1985, no. 3.
Gallemore, Jr. J.L. and Panton, J.H. *Inmate responses to lengthy death row confinement.* American Journal of Psychiatry. Washington, D.C., 129 : 167-172, 1972, no. 2. Also in Capital punishments in the United States. Edited by H.A. Bedau and C.M. Pierce, New York, N.Y. AMS Press, 1976, p. 527-534.
Gallup, G. *The death penalty.* Gallup Reports, Princeton, NJ, 244-245 : 10-16, January-February 1986.
Gamser, D. and Jankovic, I. *Stravovi sudija o smrtnoj kazni (The attitudes of judges towards capital punishment).* Socioloski Pregled. Beograd, 16 : 63-74, 1982, no. 3.
Garcia Valdés, C. *No a la pena de muerte (No to the death penalty). Madrid, Edicusa, 1975, 321 p.*
Gardiner, G. Capital punishment as a deterrent : and the alternative. London, Victor Gollancz Ltd., 1956.
Gardiner, G. *Criminal law ; capital punishment in Britain.* American Bar Association Journal. Chicago, IL, 45 : 259-261, March 1959.
Gardiner, G. and Curtis-Raleigh, N. *The judicial attitude to penal reform.* Law Quarterly Review. London, 65, April 1949.
Gardiner, G., Glover, E. and Mannheim, H. *A symposium on the report of the Royal Commission on Capital Punishment.* British Journal of Delinquency, London, 4 : 158-172, January 1954.
Gardner, E.S. *The Court last resort.* New York, N.Y., W. Sloane Associates, 1952.
Gardner, E.S. *Helping the innocent.* UCLA Law Review. Los Angeles, CA, 17 : 535-541, 1970.
Gardner, M. *Mormanism and capital punishment.* Dialogue : a Journal of Morman Thought. Arlington, VA, 12 : 9-26, 1979.
Gardner, M.R. *Executions and indignities : an eighth amendment assessment of methods of inflicting capital punishment.* Ohio State Law Journal. Columbus, OH, 39 : 96-130, 1978, no. 1.
Gardner, R.L. *Capital punishment : the philosophers and their court.* Syracuse Law Review. Syracuse, N.Y., 29 : 1175-1216, Fall 1978.
Gardner v. Florida : *The application of due process to sentencing procedures.* Vanderbilt Law Review. Nashville, TN, 63 : 1281, 1977.
Garey, M. *The cost of taking life : dollars and the sense of the death penalty.* University of California Davis Law Review. Davis, CA, 18 : 1221-1274, 1985.
Garret, S.M. People v. Murtishaw : *Applying the Frye test to psychiatric predictions of dangerousness in capital cases.* California Law Review. Berkeley, CA, 70 : 1069-1090, 1982, no. 4.
Gaudemet, J. *Le problème de la responsabilité pénale dans l'antiquité (The problem of criminal liability in ancient times). In* Studi in onore di Emilio Betti, vol. II, Milan, A. Giuffré, 1961.
Geimer, W. *Death at any cost : a critique of the Supreme Court's recent retreat from its death penalty standards.* Florida State University Law Review. Tallahassee, FL, 12 : 737-780, 1985.

Geis, G. *The death penalty in Oklahoma.* Proceedings of the Oklahoma Academy of Science. Norman, OK, 34 : 191-193, 1953.
Gelbert, P. *L'exécution des codamnés à mort en Grèce antique (Executions in ancient Greece).* Revue Internationale de Criminologie et de Police Technique. Genève : 38-39, 1948.
Gelles, R.J. and Strauss M.A. *Family experience and public support of the death penalty. American Journal of Orthopsychiatry.* Albany, N.Y., 45 : 596-613, 1975, no. 4. Also in Capital punishment in the United States. Edited by H.A. Bedau and C.M. Pierce, New York, N.Y., AMS Press, 1976.
Gerber, R.J. *Death penalty we can live with.* Notre Dame Lawyer. Notre Dame, IN, 50 : 251-272, December 1974.
Gerstein, R.M. *A prosecutor looks at capital punishment. Journal of Criminal Law, Criminology and Police Science.* Baltimore, MD, 51 : 252-257, July-August 1960.
Gerstein, R.S. *Capital punishment – Cruel and unusual ? A retributivist response.* Ethics. Chicago, IL, 85 : 75-79, 1974, no. 1.
Gettinger, S.H. *Death row in America.* Corrections Magazine. New York, N.Y., 2 : 37-48, 1976, no. 5.
Gettinger, S.H. *Sentenced to die : the people, the crimes, and the controversy.* New York, N.Y., MacMillan, 1976, 284 p.
Giardini, G. and Farrow, R.G. *The paroling of capital offenders.* Annals of the American Academy of Political and Social Sciences. Philadelphia, PA, no. 284 : 85-94, 1952.
Gibbs, J.P. and Erickson, M.L. *Capital punishment and the deterrence doctrine. In* Capital punishment in the United States, Edited by H.A. Bedau and C.M. Pierce. New York, N.Y., AMS Press, 1976, p. 299-313.
Gibbs, J.P. and Erickson, M.L. *Crime, punishment, and deterrence.* New York, N.Y., Elsevier, 1975.
Gibbs, J.P. and Erickson, M.L. *A critique of the scientific literature on capital punishment and deterrence.* Journal of Behavioral Economics. Macomb, IL, 6 : 279-310, 1977.
Gibbs, J.P. and Erickson, M.L. *The death penalty : retribution and penalty policy.* Journal of Criminal Law and Criminology. Baltimore, MD, 69 : 291-199, 1978, no. 3.
Gibbs, J.P. and Erickson, M.L. *Preventive effects of capital punishment other than deterrence.* Criminal Law Bulletin. Boston, MA, 14 : 34-50, 1978, no. 1. Also in The death penalty in America. Edited by H.A. Bedau, 3rd ed. Oxford. Oxford University Press, 1982, p. 103-115.
Gillers, S. *Deciding who dies.* University of Pennsylvania Law Review. Philadelphia, PA, 129 : 1-124, 1980, no. 1.
Gillers, S. *The quality of mercy : costitutional accuracy at the selection state of capital sentencing.* University of California Davis Law Review. Davis, CA, 18 : 1037-1112, 1985.
Gilloon, T.J. *Capital punishment and the burden of proof : the sentencing decision.* California Western Law Review. San Diego, CA, 17 : 316-353, 1981, no. 2.
Ginsberg, W.R. *Punishment of capital offenders : a critical examination of the Connecticut Statute.* Connecticut Bar Journal. Hartford, CT, 27 : 273-281, 1953.

Girsh, F.J. *The Witherspoon question : the social science and the evidence.* National Legal Aid and Defender Association Briefcase. Washington, D.C., 35 : 99-125, 1978, no. 4.

Glaser, D. *Capital punishment – Deterrent or stimulus to murder ? Our unexamined deaths and penalties.* University of Toledo Law Review. Toledo, OH, 10 : 317-333, 1979, no. 2.

Glaser, D. *The realities of homicide versus the assumptions of economists in assessing capital punishment.* Journal of Behavioral Economics; Macomb, IL, 6 : 243-268, 1977.

Glaser, D. *A response to Bailey – More evidence on capital punishment as correlate of tolerance for murder.* Crime and Delinquency. Hackensack, N.J., 22 : 40-43, January 1976.

Glaser, D. and Zeigler, M.S. *Use of the death penalty v. outrage at murder.* Crime and Delinquency. Hackensack, N.J., 20 : 333-338, October 1974.

Glover, E. *Psychiatric aspects of the report on capital punishment.* Modern Law Review. London, 17, July 1954.

Goetz, R.J. *Should Ohio abolish capital punishment ?* Cleveland Marshall Law Review. Cleveland, OH, 10 : 365-377, May 1961.

Gold, L.H. *A psychiatric review of capital punishment.* Journal of Forensic Sciences. Chicago, IL, 6 : 465-478, October 1961.

Goldberg, A.J. and Dershowitz, A.M. *Declaring the death penalty unconstitutional.* Harvard Law Review. Cambridge, MA, 83 : 1773-1819, June 1970.

Goldberg, F. *Toward expansion of Witherspoon in capital scruples jury bias, and the use of psychological data to raise presumptions in the law.* Harvard Civil Rights Civil Liberties Review. Cambridge, Ma, 5 : 53-69, 1970.

Goldberg, S. *On capital punishment.* Ethics. Chicago, IL, 85 : 67-74, 1974, no. 1.

Goldstein, A. *Unquiet death of Julius and Ethel Rosenberg.* Los Angeles, CA, Lawrence Hill, 1974, 96 p.

Gomez de la Torre, I.B. *The death penalty in current Latin American law. In* International summaries vol. 2. Washington, D.C., National Institute of Law Enforcement and Criminal Justice, 1978, p. 19-25.

Goodpaster, G. *Judicial review of death sentences.* Journal of Criminal Law and Criminology. Chicago, IL, 74 : 786-826, 1983, no. 3.

Goodpaster, G. *Trial for life : effective assistance of counsel.* New York University Law Review. New York, N.Y., 58 : 299-362, 1983.

Gordon, R.W. *Crystal-balling death ?* Baylor Law Review. Waco, TX, 30 : 35-64, 1976, no. 1.

Gorecki, J. *Capital punishment : criminal law and social evolution.* New York, N.Y., Columbia University Press, 1983, 165 p.

Gottlieb, G.H. *Capital punishment.* Crime and Delinquency. Hackensack, N.J., 15 : 1-20, January 1969.

Gottlieb, G.H. *Is the death penalty unconstitutional ? In* The death penalty in America ; an anthology. Edited by H.A. Bedau. Garden City, N.Y., Anchor Books, 1964, 584 p.

Gottlieb, G.H. *Testing the death penalty.* Southern California Law Review. Los Angeles, CA, 34 : 268-281, Spring 1961.
Gova Garcia, L. *Proyecto de ley de régimen de ejecucion de la pena : Es o no es eficaz la pena de muerte para la extincion del delito ? (Draft law on the execution of punishment : is the death penalty a crime deterrent or not ?) In* Actes du IIe Contrès International de Criminologie, vol. 4. Paris. Presses Universitaires, 1953, p. 600-662.
Gowers, E. *A life for a life ? The problem of capital punishment.* London, Chatto and Windus, 1956, 144 p.
Grajewski, H. *Kara śmierci w prawie polskim do polowy XIV wieku (The death penalty in Polish law up to the middle of the XIV Century).* Warszawa, 1956.
Graven, J. A propos d'un procès retentissant et d'un récent référendum sur la peine de mort (On a trial of great interest and a recent referendum on the death penalty). Revue Internationale de Criminologie et de Police Technique. Genève : 1-16, 1958.
Graven, J. *Les conceptions pénales et l'actualité de Montesquieu (Criminological ideas and the actuality of Montesquieu).* Revue de Droit Pénal et de Criminologie, Bruxelles : 161, 1949-1950.
Graven, J. *Nouvelles reflexions sur la peine capitale (New reflections on the death penalty). In* Recueil d'études en hommage à la mémoire du Professeur Henri Donnedieu de Vabres. Paris, Cujas, 1960, p. 231-254.
Graven, J. *Peut-on se passer de la peine de mort ? (Can we live without the death penalty ?) In* Pena de Morte. Coloquio Internacional Comemorativo do Centenario da Abolicao da Penal de Morte em Portugal, vol. II. Coimbra, Faculdade de Direito, Universidade de Coimbra, 1967, p. 229-271.
Graven, J. *Le problème de la peine de mort (The problem of the death penalty).* Bulletin de la Société Internationale de Criminologie. Paris, 1st/2nd : 13-27, 1953.
Graven, J. *Le problème de la peine de mort et sa réapparition en Suisse (The problem of the death penalty and its reappearance in Switzerland).* Revue Internationale de Criminologie et de Police Technique, Genève : 3-123, 1952.
Graves, W.F. *The deterrent effect of capital punishment in California. In* The death penalty in America ; an anthology. Edited by H.A. Bedau. Garden City, N.Y., Anchor Books, 1964, p. 322-332.
Graves, W.F. *A doctor looks at capital punishment.* Medical Arts and Sciences. Loma Linda, CA, 10 : 137-141, 1956, no. 4.
Gredd, H. *Washington v. Strickland : defining effective assistance of counsel at capital sentencing.* Columbia Law Review. New York, N.Y., 83 : 1544-1581, 1983, no. 6.
Green, W. *Capital punishment, psychiatric experts and predictions of dangerousness.* Campbell University Law Review. Buie's Creek, N.C., 13 : 533-553, 1984.
Greenberg, J. *Against the American system of capital punishment.* Harvard Law Review. Cambridge, MA, 99 : 1690-1680, 1986.
Greenberg, J., Greenberg, H. and Urrows, E. eds. *Capital punishment : the long road up from barbarism.* Lexington, MA, Heath, 1984.

Greenberg, J. *Capital punishment : the United States experience.* Paper presented at the meeting of Amnesty International on capital punishment during the Sixth UN Congress, August 1980. (A/Conf. 87/NGO/ULHR).
Greenberg, J. *Capital punishment as a system.* Yale Law Journal. New Haven, CT, 91 : 908-936, 1982, no. 5.
Greenberg, J. *The death penalty : where do we go from here ?* National Legal Aid and Defender Association Briefcase. Chicago, IL, 34 : 55-57, 1976-77, no. 2.
Greenberg, J. and Himmelstein, J. *Varieties of attack on the death penalty.* Crime and Delinquency. Hackensack, N.J., 15 : 112-120, January 1969.
Greenwald, H.B. *Capital punishment for minors : an eighth amendment analysis.* Journal of Criminal Law and Criminology. Chicago, IL, 74 : 1471-1517, 1983, no. 4.
Gregg v. Georgia, Proffitt v. Florida, Roberts v. Lousiana, Jurek v. Texas, Woodson v. North Carolina. *Criminal Law Reporter.* Washington, D.C., 19 : 4105-4112, July 1976, no. 16.
Grenier, B. *Capital punishment : new material 1965-72.* Ottawa, Ont., 1972, 161 p.
Griffiths, A.R.G. *Capital punishment in South Australia, 1836-1964.* Australia and New Zealand Journal of Criminology. Melbourne, 3 : 214-222, December 1970.
Griggs, L. *Harmless error, cause and prejudice, comity and federalism : « Legal magic » and the Florida death penalty.* Stetson Law Review (De Land, FL), 13 : 83-114, 1983.
Grinnel, F.W. *The jury and death sentences.* Massachusetts Law Quarterly, Boston, MA, 31 : 60-61, October 1946.
Gross, F.A. *Who hangs the hangman ? A modern approach to punishment.* Cape Town, 1966, 198 p.
Gross, S.R. *Determining the neutrality of death-qualified juries. Judicial appraisal of empirical data.* Law and Human Behavior. New York, N.Y., 8 : 7-30, 1984, no. 1/2.
Gross, S.R. and Mauro, R. *Patterns of death : an analysis of racial disparities in capital sentencing and homicide victimization.* Stanford Law Review. Stanford, CA, 37 : 27-153, 1984, no. 1.
Gross, S.R. *Race and death : the judicial evaluation of evidence of discrimination in capital sentencing.* University of California Davis Law Review. Davis, CA, 18 : 1275-1386, 1985.
Grunhut, M. *Murder and the death penalty in England.* Annals of the American Academy of Political and Social Science. Philadelphia, PA : 158-166, November 1952.
Grzéskowiak, A. *Capital punishment in Polish penal law.* Crime Prevention and Criminal Justice Newsletter. Vienna no. 12/13 : 43-46, November 1986.
Grzéskowiak, A. and Sliwowski, G. *The death penalty in the new Polish criminal legislation. In* International summaries. vol. 2. Washington, D.C., National Institute of Law Enforcement and Criminal Justice, 1978, p. 1-9.
Grzéskowiak, A. *Idea abolicjonizmu na tle wspolczesnych systemów prawnokarnych (Abolitionist ideas in contemporary penal systems).* Kósciól i Prawo. Lublin, 5, 1986.

Grzéskowiak, A. *Kara śmierci w polskim prawie karnym (The death penalty in Polish law).* Torun, Univ. Mikolaja Kopernika, 1982, 292 p.
Grzéskowiak, A. and G. Sliwowski, G. *La peine de mort dans la nouvelle législation criminelle polonaise (The death penalty in the new Polish criminal law).* Revue Pénitentiaire et de Droit Pénal. Paris, n° 2 : 227-235, avril-juin 1977.
Grzéskowiak, A. *Ruch abolicjonistów wloskich w II polowie XIX wieku (The Italian abolistionist movement in the second half of the XIX century).* Acta Universitatis Nicolai Copernici. Torun, 16 : 165-179, 1978.
Grzéskowiak, A. *Znieść kare śmierci ! (Abolish the death penalty !)* Palestra. Warsaw, no. 9-10 : 59-67, 1982.
Guillot, E.E. *Abolition and restoration of the death penalty in Missouri. In* The death penalty in America ; an anthology. Edited by H.A. Bedau. Garden City, N.Y., Anchor Books, 1964, p. 351-359.
Guizot, F. *De la peine de mort en matière politique (On the death penalty regarding political matters).* Paris, Béchet, 1822.
Haag, E. *On deterrence and the death penalty.* Journal of Criminal Law, Criminology and Police Science. Baltimore, MD, 60 : 141-147, 1969, no. 2.
Haas, F. *Putting the death penalty on trial for its life.* Boston Phoenix. Boston, MA, 4 : 6 and 14, 13 May 1975.
Hadar, Z. *Communication.* Military Law and Law of War Review. Brussels, 11 : 147-152, 1972, no. 1.
Hagerty, W.B. *Capital punishment should be retained.* Canadian Bar Journal, Ottawa, Ont., 3 : 42-51, 1960.
Hahlo, H.R. *Scandalizing justice : the Van Niekerk story.* University of Toronto Law Journal. Toronto, Ont., 21 : 378-392, 1971, no. 3.
Hale, L. *Hanged in error.* Harmondsworth, Penguin Books, 1961, 160 p.
Haller, K. *Capital punishment statutes after Furman.* Ohio State Law Journal. Columbus, OH, 35 : 651-685, 1974, no. 3.
Hamilton, V.L. and Rotkin, L. *The capital punishment debate : public perceptions of crimes and punishment.* Journal of Applied Social Psychology. Silver Spring, MD, 9 : 350-376, 1979, no. 4.
Hamilton, V.L. and Rotkin, L. *Interpreting the eighth amendment : perceived seriousness of crime and severity of punishment. In* Capital punishment in the United States. Edited by H.A. Bedau and C.M. Pierce. New York, N.Y., AMS Press, 1976, p. 502-526.
Hammer, R. *Between life and death.* Toronto, Ont., MacMillan Company, 1969.
Han, W. *China's experience with the death penalty : no abolition now, only minimization.* Crime Prevention and Criminal Justice Newsletter. Vienna, no. 12/13 : 25-26, November 1986.
Handa, R.L. *Capital punishment.* Indian Journal of Criminology. Madras, 12 : 1-2, 1964, no. 1.
Handberg, R. *C.M. Unkovic and R. Wright. Crime, punishment and deterrence : the impact of an execution on attitudes toward the death penalty.* Indian Journal of Criminology. Mandras, 11 : 18-32, 1983, no. 1.
Haney, C. *Evolving standards and the capital jury.* Law and Human Behavior. New York, N.Y., 8 : 153-160, 1984, no. 1/2.
Haney, C. *Examining death qualification.* Further analysis of the process

effect. Law and Human Behavior. New York, N.Y., 8 : 133-151, 1984, no. 1/2.
Haney, C. *Juries and the death penalty : readdressing the Witherspoon question.* Crime and Delinquency. Hackensack, N.J., 26 : 512-527, 1980, no. 4.
Haney, C. *On the selection of capital juries.* The biasing effects of the death-qualification process. Law and Human Behavior. New York, N.Y., 8 : 121-132, 1984, no. 1/2.
Hankins, L. (as told to Earle Guy). *Nineteen years innocent.* New York, N.Y., Exposition Press, 1956, 110 p.
Hann, R.G. Deterrence and the death penalty. Ottawa, Ont., Ministry of the Solicitor General, 1975 and 1977.
Hardman, D.G. *Notes at an unfinished lunch.* Crime and Delinquency. Hackensack, N.J., 23 : 365-371, October 1977.
Harley, H. *Segregation versus hanging.* Journal of Criminal Law, Criminology and Police Science. Baltimore, MD, 11 : 512-527, February 1921.
Harremoes, E. *The Council of Europe and its efforts to promote the abolition of the death penalty.* Crime Prevention and Criminal Justice Newsletter. Vienna, no. 12/13 : 62-64, November 1986.
Harremoes, E. *Langstrafer.* Bewaehrungshilfe. Bonn, 25 : 93-99, 1978, no. 2.
Harrison, E. and Prather, A.V.J. *No time for dying.* Englewood Cliffs, N.J., Prentice-Hall, Inc., 1973, 259 p.
Hart, H.L.A. *Punishment and responsibility.* London, Oxford University Press, 1968, 271 p.
Hartmann, R. *The use of lethal gas in Nevada executions.* St. Louis University Law Journal. St. Louis, MO, 8 : 164-168, April 1923.
Hartung, F.E. *Trends in the use of capital punishment.* Annals of the American Academy of Political and Social Science. Philadelphia, PA, 284 : 8-20, November 1952.
Hawkins, G. *Punishment and deterrence : the educative, moralizing, and habituative effects. In* Theories of punishment. Edited by S.L. Gruppo. Bloomington, IN, Indiana University Press, 1971, p. 163-180.
Hayner, N.S. and Cranor, J.R. *The death penalty in Washington State.* Annals of the American Academy of Political and Social Science. Philadelphia, PA, 284 : 101-105, November 1952.
Hearn, P.J.O. *Criminal law – Capital punishment, corporal punishment and lotteries. Joint Committee Reports.* Canadian Bar Review. Downsview, Ont.), 34 : 844-855, 1956.
Hellwig, L.G. *The death penalty in Washington : a historical perspective.* Washington Law Review. Seattle, WA, 57 : 525-549, 1982, no. 3.
Henry, W. *Representation of death sentenced inmates.* Florida Bar Journal. Tallahassee, FL, 59 : 53-56, November 1985.
Herrmann, J. and Marty, D.F. *Vers l'abolition de la peine de mort aux Etats-Unis ? (Towards the abolition of capital punishment in the U.S.A. ?)* Revue de Droit Pénal et de Criminologie. Bruxelles, 53 : 831-844, juin 1973.
Hester, R.K. and Smith, R.E. *Effects of a mandatory death penalty on the decisions of simulated jurors as a function of heinousness of the crime.* Journal of Criminal Justice. Bloomington, IN, 1 : 319-326, 1973, no. 4.

Hibbert, C. *The roots of evil.* Boston, Little, Brown and Co., 1963.
Hill, C.M. *Can the death penalty be imposed on juveniles : the unanswered question* in Eddings v. Oklahoma. Criminal Law Bulletin. Boston, MA, 20 : 5-33, 1984, no. 1.
Hill, D. and Pond, D.A. *Reflections on one-hundred capital cases submitted to electroencephalography.* Journal of Mental Science. London, 98 : 23-43, January 1952.
Hilliard, E.G. *Capital punishment in Ohio : aggravating circumstances.* Cleveland State Law Review. Cleveland, OH, 31 : 495-528, 1982, no. 3.
Hivert, P. *La peine de mort, pour quoi faire ? (The death penalty, what for ?)* Revue Pénitentiaire et de Droit Pénal. Paris, no. 4 : 617-619, octobre-décembre 1979.
Hochkammer, W.O. *The capital punishment controversy.* Journal of Criminal Law, Criminology and Police Science. Baltimore, MD, 60 : 360-368, September 1969.
Hodge, D.M. Flanagan v. Watson et al. *Massachusetts state death penalty statute held unconstitutional – Legal decision or moral choice of the justices ?* New England Journal on Prison Law. Boston, MA, 7 : 429-470, 1981, no. 2.
Hoenack, S.A., Kurdle, R. and Squist, D. *The deterrent effect of capital punishment : a question of identification.* Policy Analysis. New York, N.Y. : 489-527, Fall 1978.
Hoenack, S.A. and Weiler, W.C. *A structural model of murder behavior and the criminal justice system.* American Economic Review. Nashville, TN, 70 : 327-341, 1980, no. 3.
Hogan, B. *The killing ground : 1964-73.* Criminal Law Review. London : 387-401, July 1974.
Hogarth, J. *Sentencing as a human process.* Toronto, Ont., University of Toronto Press, 1972.
Hook, S. *The death sentence. In* The death penalty in America ; an anthology. Edited by H.A. Bedau. Garden City, N.Y., Anchor Books, 1964, p. 146-154.
Hoover, J.E. *Statements in favor of the death penalty. In* The death penalty in America ; an anthology. Edited by H.A. Bedau. Garden City, N.Y., Anchor Books, 1964, p. 130-135.
Hope-Wallace, P. *Half-hearted abolitionist. In* The hanging question. Edited by L. Blom-Cooper. London, Duckworth and Co., 1969, p. 63-66.
Horoszewicz, M. Kosciol rzymski i kara smierci (The catholic church and the death penalty). Czlowiek i Swiatopoglad, no. 7 : 4-34, 1983.
Horowitz, I.A. and Seguin, D.G. *The effects of bifurcation and death qualification on assignment of penalty in capital crimes.* Journal of Applied Social Psychology. Silver Spring, MD, 16 : 165-185, 1986, no. 2.
Horváith, T. *A Halabüntetés a szocialista országok büntetésjogában.* Allam-és Jogtudomany : 529-530, 1975, no. 4.
Horwitz, E.L. *Capital punishment U.S.A.* Philadelphia, PA, Lippincott Co., 1973, 192 p.
House Bill 200 : the legislative attempt to reinstate capital punishment in Texas. Houston Law Review. Houston, TX, 11 : 410-423, January 1974.
Hubbard, J.P. *Reasonable levels of arbitrariness in death sentencing pat-*

terns : a tragic perspective on capital punishment. University of California Davis Law Review. Davis, CA, 18 : 1113-1165, 1985.
Huffman, R.D. *Witherspoon after Wheeler : death qualifying is bad for defendant.* Criminal Justice Journal. San Diego, CA, 3 : 1-22, 1979, no. 1.
Hugo, V. *Ecrits de Victor Hugo sur la peine de mort (Essays by Victor Hugo on the death penalty).* Edités par R. Jean. Maussan les Alpilles, Actes/Sud, 1979, 244 p.
Huie, W.B. *The execution of Private Slovik.* New York, N.Y., Dell Publishing Co. Inc., 1971, 250 p.
Hulsman, L.H.C. *Choix de la sanction pénale (The choice of punishment).* Revue de Science Criminelle et de Droit Pénal Comparé. Paris, no. 3 : 497-545, juillet-septembre 1970.
Hungria, N. *A pena de morte no Brasil (The death penalty in Brazil).* Revista Brasileira de Criminologia e Direito Penal. Rio de Janeiro, no. 17 : 7-20, abril-junio 1967.
Husbands, R.H. *New direction for capital sentencing or an about-face for the Supreme Court ?* Lockett v. Ohio. A recent development. American Criminal Law Review. Washington, D.C., 16 : 317-337, 1979, no. 3.
Hyatt Williams, A. *Murderousness. In* The hanging question. Edited by L. Blom-Cooper. London. Duckworth and Co., 1969, p. 91-100.
Ibrahimpasic, B. *O smrtnoj kazni u sistemu krivicnopravnih sankcija socijalisteckog drustva (The death penalty in the socialist system of penal sanctions).* Pregled. Sarajevo, 18 : 269-279, 1966.
Ignatow, A.N. and Osipow, P.P. *Rol ugolowno-prawowjch sankcji w prieduprezdenii priestuplenij (The role of penal sanctions in the prevention of crime).* Wiestnik Leningradskogo Uniwiersiteta. Leningrad, 5 : 65, 1981.
Iida, T. *(Suspension of execution of the death sentence).* Horitsu jiho. Japan, 42 : 38, May 1970, In Japanese.
Imbert, J. *La peine de mort (The death penalty).* Paris, Librairie Armand Colin, 1967, 207 p.
Imbert, J. *La peine de mort et l'opinion au XVIIIe siècle (The death penalty and public opinion in the XVIIIth century).* Paris : 509-525, juillet-septembre 1964.
" Inform or die " in Rhodesia. Review – International Commission of Jurists. Geneva, no. 11 : 11, December 1973.
Ingram, T.E. ed. *Essays on the death penalty.* Houston, TX, St. Thomas Press, 1963.
Innerst, J.S. and Manice, E.A. *Capital punishment. In* Report of a Conference of Freinds from the United States and Canada. Philadelphia, PA, Freinds World Committee, 1959, p. 44-48.
Innerst, J.S. *Is capital punishment the answer ?* Richmond, IN, Board of Peace and Social Concerns, The Five Years Meeting of Friends, 1959, 6 p.
Insanity of the condemned. Yale Law Journal. New Haven, CT, 88 : 533-564, 1979.
International AI conference on death penalty adopts declaration of Stockholm. Amnesty International Newsletter. London, 8 : 1, January 1978.
Irvin, C. and Rose H.E. *The response to Furman : can legislators breathe life back into death ?* Cleveland State Law Review. Cleveland, OH, 23 : 172-189, 1974, no. 1.

Is the death penalty dead ? Baylor Law Review. Waco, TX, 26 : 114-122, Winter 1974.
Is there any evidence that hanging deters killers ? New Society. London, 48 : 759-761, 28 June 1979.
Isenberg, I. ed. *Death penalty.* New York, N.Y., H.W. Wilson Company, 1977, 161 p.
Ita, T.A. *Habeas corpus – expedited appellate review of habeas corpus petitions brought by death-sentenced state prisoners.* Barefoot v. Estelle, 103 S. Ct. 3383 (1983). Journal of Criminal Law and Criminology. Chicago, IL, 74 : 1404-1424, no. 4.
Jackson, B. and Christian, D. *Death row.* Boston, MA, Beacon Press, 1980, 292 p.
Jacoby, J.E. and Paternoster R. *Sentencing disparity and jury packing : further challenges to the death penalty.* Journal of Criminal Law and Criminology. Chicago, IL, 73 : 379-387, 1982, no. 1.
Jacques, P. *Pena de morte a colônias correcionais (Capital punishment and penal colonies).* Revista de Informaçâo Legislativa. Brasilia, 21 : 131-134, no. 82.
Jadhav, U.K. *Is capital punishment necessary ?* Khar, Bombay, Anand Publications, 1972.
Jamaica. *Death sentence on defendants aged 18 for murder committed when under that age – Whether unconstitutional.* Criminal Law Review. London : 49-50, January 1976.
James, L. *Hanging : the aftermath.* Justice of the Peace. Chichester, Sussex, 147 : 552-553, 1983, no. 35.
Jankovic, I. *Argumenti protiv smrtne kazne (Arguments against capital punishment).* Dometi. Rijeka : 72-86, 1983, no. 12.
Jankovic, I. *O kazni protiv smrtne kazne (On the penalty of the death sentence).* Socioloski Pregled. Beograd, nos. 3/4, 1980.
Jankovic, I. *Nesto o smrtnoj kazni (Notes on the death penalty).* Beograd, nos. 3/4, 1981.
Jankovic, I. *Socialism and the death penalty. In* Research in law, deviance and social control : a research annual. vol. 6. Edited by S. Spiyzer and A.T. Scull. Greenwich, CT, Jai Press, Inc., 1984, p. 243-264.
Jankovic, I. *Smrt u prisustvu vlasti : smrtna kazna u jogoslaviji i svetu (Death in the presence of the authorities : capital punishment in Yugoslavia and abroad).* Beograd, ICSSO Srbije, 1985, 250 p.
Jasinski, J. *Gos przeciw karze śmierci (Voices against the death penalty).* Państwo i Prawo. Warsaw, no. 9-12 : 85-90, 1981.
Jasinski, J. *Kara śmierci w aspekcie prawngm i moralnym (Legal and moral aspects of the death penalty).* Wieź, 12 : 85-90, 1981.
Jayasuriya, D.C. *Penal measures for drug offences : perspectives from some Asian countries.* Bulletin on Narcotics. Colombo, 36 : 9-13, 1984, no. 3.
Jayewardene, C.H.S. *Canadian experiment with the death penalty.* Ottawa, Ont., University of Ottawa, 1973.
Jayewardene, C.H.S. *The Canadian movement against the death penalty.* Canadian Journal of Criminology and Corrections. Ottawa, Ont., 14 : 366-390, October 1972.
Jayewardene, C.H.S. *The death penalty and the safety of Canadian poli-*

cemen. Canadian Journal of Criminology and Corrections. Ottawa, Ont., 15 : 356-366, October 1973.
Jayewardene, C.H.S. *The death penalty in Ceylon.* Ceylon Journal of Historical and Social Studies. Peradeniya, 3 : 166-186, 1961.
Jayewardene, C.H.S. *Life or death. Society's reaction to murder ?* Canadian Journal of Criminology and Corrections. Ottawa, Ont., 15 : 265-273, 1973, no. 3.
Jayewardene, C.H.S. *The penalty of death. The Canadian experiment.* Lexington, MA, D.C. Heath, 1978.
Jayewardene, C.H.S. *The public opinion argument in the death penalty debate.* Canadian Journal of Criminology. Ottawa, Ont., 22 : 404-411, 1980, no. 4.
Jayewardene, C.H.S. and Singh, A. *Public opinion polls on the death penalty.* Psychological Reports. Missoula, MT, 44 : 1191-1195, 1979, no. 3.
Jensen, S.G. *Debatten om dodsstraf (Debates on capital punishment).* Nordisk Tidsskrift for Kriminalvidenskab. Kobenhavn, 50 : 396-403, 1962, no. 3/4.
Jensen, S.G. *Studier over lovens strengeste straf i Danmark 1858-1957.* Kobenhavn, 1974, 119 p.
Jescheck, H.H. *The death penalty. In* Crime, criminology and public policy. Edited by R. Hood. London, Heinemann Educational Books Ltd., 1974, p. 511-512.
Jester, J.C. *The abolition of public executions : a case study.* International Journal of Criminology and Penology. London, 4 : 25-32, Februry 1976.
Johanson, B.O. *Capital Punishment.* Journal of Contemporary Roman-Dutch Law (South Africa), 34 : 350, November 1971.
Johnson, E.H. *Executions and commutations in North Carolina. In* The death penalty in America ; an anthology. Edited by H.A. Bedau. Garden City, N.Y., Anchor Books, 1964, p. 452-463.
Johnson, E.H. *Selective factors in capital punishment.* Social Forces. Chapel Hill, N.C., 36 : 165-169, December 1957.
Johnson, G. and Newmeyer J. *Pleasure, punishment and moral indignation.* Sociology and Social Research. Los Angeles, CA, 59 : 82-95, 1975, no. 2.
Johnson, J.E. *The supreme penalty goes on trial.* Police Review. London, no. 4479 : 1702-1704, November 1978.
Johnson, J.E. ed. *Capital punishment.* New York, N.Y., H.W. Wilson Co., 1939, 262 p.
Johnson, K.L. *The death row right to die : suicide or intimate decision.* Southern California Law Review. Los Angeles, CA, 54 : 575-631, 1981, no. 3.
Johnson, R. *Condemned to die : life under sentence of death.* New York, N.Y., Emsevier-North Holland, 1981, 190 p.
Johnson, R. *Under sentence of death : the psychology of death row confinement.* Law and Psychology Review. University, AL, no. 5 : 141-192, Fall 1979.
Johnson, R. *Warehousing for death.* Observations on the human environment of death row. Crime and Delinquency. Hackensack, N.J., 26 : 545-562, 1980, no. 4.

Johnston, N., Savitz, L. and Wolfgang, M.E. eds. *The sociology of punishment and correction : a book of readings.* New York, N.Y., John Wiley and Sons, 1962.
Jolly, R.W. Jr. and Sagarin, E. *The first eight after Furman : who was executed with the return of the death penalty ?* Crime and Delinquency. Hackendack, N.J., 30 : 610-6623, 1984, no. 4.
Jones, B. ed. *The penalty is death.* Melbourne, Sun Books, 1968.
Jones, E. *The last two to hang.* London, MacMillan, 1966.
Jones, G. *Federal procedural implications* of Furman v. Georgia : what rights for the formerly capital offender ? American Journal of Criminal Law. Austin, TX, 1 : 318, October 1972.
Jones, H. and Potter N. *Deterrence, retribution, denunciation and the death penalty.* University of Missouri – Kansas City Law review. Kansas City, MO, 49 : 158-169, 1981, no. 2.
Jovane, E. *Carcere a vita e pena di morte.* Rassegna di Studi Penitenziari. Roma, no. 6 : 625-628, novembre-dicembre 1964.
Joyce, J.A. *Capital punishment : a world view.* New York, N.Y., Thomas Nelson and Sons, 1961.
Joyce, J.A. *The right to life : a world view of capital punishment.* London, Victor Gollancz Ltd., 1962.
Judson, C., Pandell, J. and Owens, J. *A study of the penalty jury in first degree murder cases.* Stanford Law review. Stanford, CA, 21 : 1297-1431, 1969.
Junker, J.M. *Death penalty cases : a preliminary comment.* Washington Law Review. Seattle, WA, 48 : 95-109, November 1972.
Junod, H.P. *Le bourreau, exécuteur des hautes œuvres (The executioner, doer of great deeds).* Revue Internationale de Criminologie et de Police Technique. Genève, no. 1 : 89-107, janvier-mars 1966.
Jurow, G.L. *New data on the effect of a " death qualified " jury on the guilt determination process.* Harvard Law Review (Cambridge, MA, 84 : 567-612, January 1971. Also in Capital punishment in the United States. Edited by H.A. Bedau and C.M. Pierce. New York, N.Y., AMS Press, 1976, p. 451-501.
Jury discretion and the unitary trial procedure in capital cases. Arkansas Law Review. Fayetteville, AR, 26 : 33, Spring 1972.
Jury selection and the death penalty : Witherspoon. Witherspoon v. Illinois. University of Chicago Law Review. Chicago, IL, 37 : 759, Summer 1970.
Kadane, J.B. *After Hovey. A note on taking account of the automatic death penalty jurors.* Law and Human Behavior. New York, N.Y., 8 : 115-120, 1984, no. 1/2.
Kahn, E. *Death penalty in South Africa.* Journal of Contemporary Roman-Dutch Law. South Africa, 33 : 108, May 1970.
Kaine, T. *Capital punishment and the waiver of sentence review.* Harvard Civil Rights – Civil Liberties Law Review. Cambridge, MA, 18 : 483-524, 1983, no. 2.
Kaiser, G. *Capital punishment in a criminological perspective.* Crime Prevention and Criminal Justice Newsletter. Vienna, no. 12/13 : 10-18, November 1986.

Kalven, H. and Zeisel, H. *The American jury.* Boston, MA, Little, Brown and Co., 1966.
Kalven, H. and Zeisel, H. *The American jury and the death penalty.* University of Chicago Law Review. Chicago, IL, 33 : 769, 1965-66.
Kanski, M. *O karze śmierci (Capital punishment).* Kracow, 1850.
Kanter, S. *Dealing with death : the constitutionality of capital punishment in Oregon.* Willamette Law Review. Salem, OR, 16 : 1-65, 1979, no. 1.
Kaplan, D. *In Florida, a story politics and death.* Nationa Law Journal. New York, N.Y., July 1984.
Kaplan, J. *Administering capital punishment.* University of Florida Law Review. Gainesville, FL, 36 : 177-192, 1984.
Kaplan, J. *Evidence in capital cases.* Florida State University Law Review. Tallahassee, FL, 11 : 369-386, 1983.
Kaplan, S.M. *Death, so say we all.* Psychology Today. New York, N.Y., 19 : 48-53, 1985, no. 7.
Karabenick, S.A., Lerner, R.M. and Beecher, M.D. *Helping behaviour and attitude congruence toward capital punishment.* Journal of Social Psychology. Provincetown, MA, 96 : 295-296, 1975, no. 2.
Karge, S.W. *Capital punishment : death for murder only.* Journal of Criminal Law and Criminology. Chicago, IL, 69 : 179-196, 1978, no. 2.
Karp, D.J. Coker v. Georgia : *disproportionate punishment and the death penalty for rape.* Columbia Law Review. New York, N.Y., 78 : 1714-1730, 1978, no. 8.
Kazis, I.J. *Judaism and the death penalty. In* The death penalty in America ; an anthology. Edited by H.A. Bedau. Garden City, N.Y., Anchor Books, 1964, p. 171-175.
Keller, D. *Die Todesstrafe in kritischer Sicht (A critical view of the death penalty).* Berlin, BRD, Walter De Gruyter and Company, 1968.
Kendall, D.E. *Constitutional attacks on the death penalty.* NLADA Briefcase. Chicago, IL, 32 : 120-124, 1975, no. 4.
Kennedy, L. *Ten Rillington Place.* New York, N.Y., Avon Books, 1971, 322 p.
Kenner, W. *Competency on death row.* International Journal of Law and Psychiatry. Elmsford, N.Y., 8 : 253-255, 1986.
Kevorkian, J. *Medical research and the death penalty.* New York, N.Y., Vantage Press, 1960, 75 p.
Kevorkian, J. *Opinions on capital punishment in the Soviet Union and its social background.* Horitsu Jiho. Japan, 42 : 53, May 1970. In Japanese.
Kida, J. *(Restoration of capital punishment in the Soviet Union and its social background).* Horitsu Jiho (Japan), 42: 53, May 1970. In Japanese.
Kikuda, K. *Capital punishment system and public opinion.* Horitsu Jiho. Japan, 42 : 43, May 1970. In Japanese.
Kim, C. and LeBlang, T.R. *Death penalty in traditional China.* Georgia Journal of International and Comparative Law. Athens, GA, 5 : 77-105, Winter 1975.
Kim, R.C. *Capital punishment : time for a stand.* Journal of Church and State. Waco, TX, 7 : 226-238, 1965, no. 2.
King, D.R. *The brutalization effect : execution publicity and the incidence*

of homicide in South Carolina. Social Forces Chapel Hill, N.C., 57 : 57 : 683-687, 1978, no. 2.

King, G.D. *On behalf of the penalty. In* The death death penalty in America. Edited by H.A. Bedau, 3rd ed. Oxford. Oxford University Press, 1982, p. 308-310.

Kingsley, R. *The case against capital punishment.* Los Angeles Bar Bulletin. Los Angeles, CA, 32 : 200-202, May 1957.

Kinney, R.R. *In defence of capital punishment.* Kentucky Law Journal. Lexington, KY, 54 : 742-757, 1966, no. 4.

Kinsolving, L. *Capital punishment : a reaction from a member of the clergy.* American Bar Association Journal. Chicago, IL, 42 : 850-852, September 1956.

Kinsolving, L. *Christianity and capital punishment.* Pastoral Psychology. Manhasset, N.Y., 11 : 33-42, June 1960.

Kirkpatrick, A.M. *The illogic of the death penalty.* Canadian Welfare. Ottawa, Ont., 47 : 14-15, 1971, no. 2.

Kirkpatrick, C. *Capital punishment.* Philadelphia, PA, Committee on Philanthropic Labor, Yearly Meeting of Friends, 1925, 55 p.

Kitz, R. and Regoli, R.M. *Police, public and capital punishment.* Journal of Crime and Justice. Jonesboro, TE, 5 : 69-85, 1982.

Klapal, C. *Vztah trestu smrti a odneti svobody (The relationship between the death penalty and the deprivation of liberty).* Prokuratura, no. 1 : 12, 1972.

Klare, H.J. *Capital punishment : an abolitionist view.* Criminologist. London, 4 : 75-82, 1969, no. 13.

Klare, H.J. *La fin de la peine capitale au Royaume-Uni (The end of capital punishment in the United Kingdom).* Revue de Droit Pénal et de Criminologie. Bruxelles : 470-471, février 1966.

Klare, H.J. *Notes on capital punishment.* London, Howard League for Penal Reform, 1963.

Klare, H.J. *La peine de mort en Angleterre en 1962 (Capital punishment in England, 1962).* Revue de Science Criminelle et de Droit Pénal Comparé. Paris : 386, 1962.

Klare, H.J. *Post-mortem on hanging.* British Journal of Criminology. London, 10 : 186-188, April 1970.

Klare, H.J. *The prison service. In* The hanging question. Edited by L. Blom-Cooper. London, Duckworth and Co., 1969, p. 115-120.

Kleck, G. *Capital punishment, gun ownership, and homicide.* American Journal of Sociology. Chicago, IL, 84 : 882-910, 1979, no. 4.

Kleck, G. *Homicide, capital punishment, and gun ownership : an aggregate analysis of U.S. homicide trends from 1947 to 1976.* Ann. Arbor, MI, University Microfilms International, 1979, 156 p.

Kleck, G. *Racial discrimination in criminal sentencing : a critical evaluation of the evidence with additional evidence on the death penalty.* American Sociological Review. Albany, N.Y., 46 : 783-804, 1981, no. 6.

Klein, L.R., Forst, B. and Filatov, V. *The deterrent effect of capital punishment : an assessment of the estimates.* Research report. Washington, D.C. National Academy of Sciences, 1976.

Klein, L.R., Forst, B. and Filatov, V. *The deterrent effect of capital punish-*

ment : an assessment of the evidence. In The death penalty in America. Edited by H.A. Bedau, 3rd ed., Oxford, Oxford University Press, 1982, p. 138-158.
Klein, R.A. *Juvenile criminals and the death penalty : resurrection of the question left unanswered in* Eddings v. Oklahoma. New England Journal on Criminal and Civil Confinement. Boston, MA, 11 : 437-487, 1985, no. 2.
Knell, B.E.F. *Capital punishment : its administration in relation to juvenile offenders in the nineteenth century and its possible administration in the eighteenth.* British Journal of Criminology. London, 5 : 198-207, 1965.
Knjazev, S. *Jos jednam o teodiceji (On theodicy again).* Zarez. Beogard, no. 2/4 : 60-65, 1983.
Knorr, S.J. *Deterrence and the death penalty : a temporal cross-sectional approach.* Journal of Criminal Law and Criminology. Chicago, IL, 70 : 235-254, 1979, no. 2.
Knowlton, R. *Problems of jury discretion in capital cases.* University of Pennsylvania Law Review. Philadelphia, PA, no. 101 : 1009, 1953.
Kobbervig, W., Inverarity, J. and Lauderdale, P. *Deterrence and the death penalty : a comment on Phillips.* American Journal of Sociology. Chicago, IL, 88 : 161-164, July 1982.
Koeninger, R.C. *Capital punishment in Texas, 1924-1968.* Crime and Delinquency. Hackensack, N.J., 15 : 132-141, January 1969.
Koestler, A. *Dialogue with death.* London, MacMillan, 1966.
Koestler, A. and Rolph, C.H. *Hanged by the neck.* Harmondsworth, Penguin Books, 1961, 143 p.
Koestler, A. *Reflections on hanging.* New York, N.Y., MacMillan Co., 1957.
Kofeod, A. *Who shall live and who shall die ?* State v. Osborn and the Idaho death penalty. Idaho Law Review. Moscow, ID, 18 : 195-213, 1982.
Kogi, S. *Etude criminologique et psychopathologique de condamnés à mort ou aux travaux forcés à perpétuité (A criminological and psychopathological study on offenders sentenced to death or to forced labour for life).* Annales Médico-Psychologiques, Paris, 2 : 377-450, 1959.
Kohlberg, L. and Elfenbein D. *The development of moral judgments concerning capital punishment.* American Journal of Orthopsychiatry. Albany, N.Y., 45 : 614-640, 1975, no. 4.
Kohlberg, L. and Elfenbein D. *Moral judgements about capital punishment : a developmental-psychological view. In* Capital punishment in the United States, Edited by H.A. Bedau and C.M. Pierce, New York, N.Y., AMS Press, 1976, p. 247-296.
Kohn, M.G. *The death penalty as presently administered under discretionary sentencing statutes is cruel and unusual punishment.* Seton Hall Law Review. Newark, N.J., 4 : 244-263, Fall-Winter 1972.
Kolly, D. Gregg v. Georgia : *the search for the civilized standard.* Detroit College of Law Review. Detroit, MI, 3 : 645-662, 1976.
Korecki, J. *Readaptacja spoleczna osob ulaskawionych od kary smierci (czy przywrocic kare dozywotniego poszbawienia wolnosci) (The social adaptation of those pardoned from death (to remain in prison for 25 years).* Panstwo i Prawo. Warsaw, n. 3/4 : 124-131, 1982.
Korff, D. *La pena de morte e il terrorismo (The death penalty and terro-*

rism). In La pena di morte nel mondo. By Amnesty International. Casale Monferrato, Marietti, 1983, p. 219-230.
Kroll, M.A. *Fighting the death penalty.* California Mawyer. San Francisco, CA, 3 : 56-58, 77, 1983, no. 6.
Kubiak, J.R. *Dzialalnosc ONZ na rzec zniesienia lub ograniczenia kary śmierci i odniesienia do praktyki w Polsce (Un activities regarding the abolition, or restriction of the use, of capital punishment and their relation to Polish practice).* Palestra, Warsaw, nos. 7-9, 1981.
Kubiak, J.R. *Kara śmierci w europejskich panstwach socjalistycznych (Capital punishment in European socialist systems).* Palestra, Warsaw, nos. 9-10 : 67-82, 1982.
Kubiak, J.R. *Przestpczość i polityka karna sadow w Czechoslowaci (Crime and criminal justice in Czechoslovakia).* Studia Prawnicze, Wroclaw, no. 1 : 224, 1983.
Kubiak, J.R. *Die Todesstrafe in einigen europaischen sozialistischen Staaten (The death penalty in some European socialist states).* Osteuropa-Recht. Stuttgart : 249-264, 1984.
Kuchty, J. and Schelleho, K. *Trest smrti vcera a dnes (The death penalty : yesterday and today).* Revue Universitatis. Brno, no. 3 : 17-23, 1982.
Kudriawcew, V.N. and Jakowlew, A.M. *Osnowanija ugolownog-prawowego zapreta (The basis of penal law prohibitions).* Moskwa, 1982.
Kumar, K. *The deterrent effects of capital punishment ; a critical analysis of arguments and evidence.* Social Defence. New Delhi, 6 : 27-35, October 1970.
Kunstler, W. *Beyond a reasonable doubt ?* Westport, CT, Greenwood Press, 1961.
Kunter, N. *Le problème de l'abolition de la peine de mort (The problem of the abolition of capital punishment).* Annales de la Faculté de droit d'Istanbul, no. 43 : 6, 1980.
Kuzma, S.M. *The constitutionality of Ohio's death penalty.* Ohio State Law Journal. Colombus, OH, 38 : 617-675, 1977, no. 3.
Kwaśniewski, J. andKojder, A. *Postawy mieszkanxow w Warszawy wobec zjawisk i zachowán dewiacyjnych (The attitudes of the citizens of Warsaw regarding deviant behaviour),* Studia Socjologiczne, Wroclaw, no. 1, 1979.
Lacassagne, A. *Peine de mort et criminalité (Capital punishment and criminality).* Paris, A. Maloine, 1906.
Lambert, L. *L'abolir... " sauf pour... " : défense de la peine de mort (abolish it... " but for... " : a defence of capital punishment).* Revue de la Police Nationale. Paris : 9-15 octobre-novembre 1971.
LaMont Smith, A. and Carter, R.M. *Count down for death.* Crime and Delinquency. Hackensack, N.J. 15 : 77-93, 1969, no. 1.
Lammich, S. *Die Sanktionen des tsechoslowakischen Strafgesetzbuches und ihre Anwendung (Punishments in the Czechoslovakian Penal Code and their application).* Zeitschrift fuer die gesamte Strafrechtwissenschaft. Berlin, BRD. 95 : 499-516, 1983, no. 2.
Lander, L. *Capital punishment as a human rights issue before the U.N.* Human Rights Journal. New York, N.Y., 4 : 511-534, 1971.
Landrove Diaz, G. *La abolición de la pena de muerte en Espana (The abo-*

lition of capital punishment in Spain). Anuario de Derecho Penal y Ciencias Penales. Madrid, 34 : 17-32, 1981, no. 1.
Landrove Diaz, G. *Las consecuencias juridicas del delito (The juridical consequences of crime).* Barcelona, Bosch, 1976, 195 p.
Lanza-Kaduce, L. *Formality, neutrality, and goal-rationality : the legacy of Weber in analyzing legal thought.* Journal of Criminal Law and Criminology. Chicago, IL, 73 : 533-560, 1982, no. 2.
Larkin, P.J. *Eighth amendment and the execution of the presently incompetent.* Stanford Law Review. Stanford, CA, 32 : 765, 1980.
Laski, H.J. *Political offences and the death penalty.* 6th Roy Calvert Memorial Lecture. London, E.G. Dunstan and Co., 1940, 11 p.
Lasky, I.I. *The paradigm of religion, medecine and capital punishment.* Medicine, Science and the Law. London, 14 : 26-31, 1974, no. 1.
Lassers, W.J. *Proof of guilt in capital cases – an unscience.* Journal of Criminal Law, Criminology and Police Science. Baltimore, MD, 58 : 310-316, 1967, no. 3.
Lassers, W.J. *Scapegoat justice : Lloyd Miller and the failure of the American legal system.* Indianapolis, IN, Indiana University Press, 1973.
Lavalette, H. de. *Moralistes et peine de mort (Moralists and capital punishment).* Etudes. Paris : 809-819, juin 1979.
LaVigne Jr., R. *Competency of jurors who have conscientious scruples against capital punishment.* Washington Law Review. Seattle, WA, 8 : 352-360, 1969, no. 3.
Lawes, L. *Futility of capital punishment.* Penal Reformer. London, 2, April 1936.
Lawes, L. *Man's judgment of death.* Montclair, N.J., Patterson-Smith, 1969, 146 p.
Lawrence, C.E. *Death as a punishment for rape – Disproportional, cruel and unusual punishment :* Coker v. Georgia. Howard Law Journal. Washington, D.C., 21 : 955-967, 1978, no. 3.
Lawrence, J. *A history of capital punishment.* New York, N.Y., Citadel Press Inc., 1960, 230 p.
Lawton, M.C. *Statement of the constitutionality of a proposed federal death penalty. In* The death penalty in America. Edited by H.A. Bedau, 3rd ed., Oxford. Oxford University Press, 1982, p. 318-322.
Layson, S. *Homicide and deterrence : another view of the Canadian time-series evidence.* Canadian Journal of Economics. Toronto, Ont., 16 : 52-73, 1983, no. 1.
Le Tourneau, p. *Plaidoyer contre la peine de mort (Pleading against capital punishment).* Cité et Justice. Paris, 6 : 89-95, 1972.
Ledewitz, B. *The new role of statutory aggravating circumstances in American death penalty law.* Duquesne Law Review. Pittsburgh, PA, 18 : 1433-1480, 1985.
Lee, S.S. *(On the abolition of capital punishment).* Pophak. Seoul, 13 : 52, December 1972. In Korean.
Legislation to suspend capital punishment. Record of the Association of the Bar of the City of New York. New York, N.Y., 27 : 390-407, 1972.
Legislative response to Furman v. Georgia : *Ohio restores the death penalty.* Akron Law Review. Akron, OH, 8 : 149-161, Fall 1974.

Legrand, A.A. *La peine de mort et les châtiments corporels applliqués aux criminels (Capital punishment and corporal punishments applied to criminals).* Archives d'Anthropologie Criminelle et de Criminologie. Paris : 689-696, 1908.
Lehtinen, M.W. *The value of life : an argument for the death penalty.* Crime and Delinquency. Hackensack, N.J., 23 : 237-252, July 1977.
Lejins, P.P. *The death penalty abroad.* Annals of the American Academy of Political and Social Science. Philadelphia, PA, 284 : 137-146, November 1952.
LeMaster, D. *The eighth amendment and Kentucky's new capital punishment provisions : waiting for the other shoe to drop.* Kentucky Law Journal. Lexington, KY, 63 : 399-429, 1974-75, no. 2.
Lempert, R. *Capital punishment in the 80's : reflections on the symposium.* Journal of Criminal Law and Criminology. Chicago, IL, 74 : 1101-1114, 1983, no. 3.
Lempert, R. *Desert and deterrence : an assessment of the moral basis of the case for capital punishment.* Michigan Law Review. Ann. Arbor, MI, 79 : 1177-1231, 1981, no. 6.
Lempert, R. *The effect of executions on homicides : a new look in an old light.* Crime and Delinquency. San Francisco, CA, 29 : 88-115, 1983, no. 1.
Leopold, N. *Life plus 99 years.* Garden City, N.Y., Doubleday, 1958, 381 p.
LeSage, C.R. *Death penalty for rape : cruel and unusual punishment.* Louisiana Law Review. Baton Rouge, LA, 38 : 868-889, 1978, no. 3.
Lester, D. *Deterring effect of executions on murder as a function of number and proportion of executions.* Psychological Reports. Missoula, MT, 45 : 598, 1979, no. 2.
Lester, D. *Executions as a deterrent to homicides.* Psychological Reports. Missoula, MT, 44 : 562, 1979, no. 2.
Lethal injection ; an uneasy alliance of law and medicine. Journal of Legal Medicine. New York, N.Y., 4 : 383-403, 1983.
Leuprecht, P. *The first international instrument for the abolition of the death penalty.* Forum. Strasbourg, no. 2 : 2-3, 1983.
Levine, H. *Death penalty and guilty pleas – Ohio Rule 11(c)(3) – A constitutional answer to a capital defendant's dilemma.* Ohio Northern University Law Review. Ada, OH, 5 : 687-718, 1978, no. 3.
Levine, M. *The adversary process and social science in the courts :* Barefoot v. Estelle. Journal of Psychiatry and Law. New York, N.Y., 12 : 147-181, 1984, no. 2.
Levine, S. *Death row : an affirmation of life.* New York, N.Y. Ballantine Books Inc., 1972, 227 p.
Levy, B. *Legacy of death.* Lexington, MA, Heath Ltd., 1973, 262 p.
Levy, E. *Die Roemische Kapitalstrafe (Roman capital punishment).* Heidelberg, Karl Winters Universitaetsbuchandlung, 1931.
Lewis, D. *Psychiatric, neurological and psychoeducational characteristics of 15 death row inmates in the United States : paper presented at the 139th Annual Meeting of the American Psychiatric Association held in Washington, D.C., May 10-16, 1986.* American Journal of Psychiatry. Washington, D.C., 143 : 838-845, 1986, no. 7.

Lewis, F.G.P. *Capital punishment : a bibliographical essay.* Toronto, Ont., Canadian Council of Churches, 1979, 45 p.

Lewis, P.W. *Killing the killers : a post* Furman profile of Florida's condemned. Crime and Delinquency. Hackensack, N.J., 25 : 200-218, 1979, no. 2.

Lewis, P.W. and Mannle, H.W. *Race and the death penalty : the victim's influence.* Journal of the American Criminal Justice Association. 41 : 47-49, 1978, no. 1.

Liebman, J.S. and Shepard, M.JU. *Guiding capital sentencing discretion beyond the " boiler plate " : mental disorder as a mitigating factor.* Georgetown Law Journal. Washington, D.C., 66 : 757-836, 1978, no. 3.

Lin, S.T. *(On the effect of the death penalty as a punishment).* Fa lu p'ing lun. China, Rep., 39 : 19, June 1973. In Chinese.

Lindsay, S. *Prosecutorial abuse of peremptory challenges in death penalty litigation : some constitutional and ethical considerations.* Campbell Law Review. Buie's Creek, N.C., 8 : 71-123, 1985.

Lipczynski, J. *Przeciwko karze smierci (Against capital punishment). In* Zagadnenia prawa karnego i teorii prawa. Warszawa, 1959, p. 91-104.

Loeb, R.H. *Crime and capital punishment.* New York, N.Y. Franklin Watts, 1978.

Loiseleur, J. *Les crimes et les peines dans l'antiquité et dans les temps modernes (Crimes and punishments in ancient and modern times).* Paris, Hachette, 1863.

Long, T.A. *Capital punishment : " cruel and unusual " ?* Ethics. Chicago, IL, 83 : 214-223, 1973, no. 3.

Lopez-Rey, M. *General overview of capital punishment as a legal sanction.* Australian Journal of Forensic Sciences. Chatswood, N.S.W., 12 : 2-10, 1979, no. 1 Also Federal Probation. Washington, D.C. : 18-23, March 1980.

Lotz, R. and Regoli, R.M. *Police, public and capital punishment.* Journal of Crime and Justice. Jonesboro, TN, 5 : 69-85, 1982.

Lotz, R. and Regoli, R.M. *Public support for the death penalty.* Criminal Justice Review. Atlanta, GA, 5 : 55-66, 1980, no. 1.

Lubert, S. *Lettre sur la peine de mort (A letter on capital punishment).* Recueil de Droit Pénal. Paris, 27 : 142-195, 1969.

Lucas, C. *Du système pénal et du système répressif en général. De la peine de mort en particulier (On criminal law and the repressive system in general. On capital punishment in particular).* Paris, Charles-Béchet, 1827.

Lucas, C. *Recueil des débats des assemblées législatives de la France sur la question de la peine de mort (French legislative assemblies on the problem of capital punishment).* Paris, 1831.

Lunde, D.T. *Our murder boom.* Psychology Today. Del Mar, CA : 35-42, July 1975.

Lunden, W.A. *The death penalty ; an analysis of capital punishment and factors related to murder.* Anamosa, IA, Iowa State Reformatory Printing Department, 1960, 28 p.

Lunden, W.A. *Is there any penalty in the death penalty ?* Ames, IA, The Art Press, 1969.

Lunden, W.A. *Time lapse between sentence and execution : the United*

States and Canada compared. American Bar Association Journal. Chicago, IL, 48 : 1043-1045, November 1962.
Lynch, P. *Scriptures and crime.* Trial. Washington, D.C. : 38/42, April-May 1965.
Le lynchage et la peine de mort (Lynching and capital punishment). Revue de Droit Pénal et de Criminologie. Bruxelles : 761, 1914-1919.
Lyons, D.B. *Capital punishment : a selected bibliography.* Criminal Law Bulletin. New York, N.Y., 8 : 783-802, 1972, no. 9.
McCafferty, J.A. *Capital punishment.* New York, N.Y., Lieber-Atherton Inc., 1973, 273 p.
McCafferty, J.A. *The death sentence and then what ?* Crime and Delinquency. Hackensack, N.J., 7 : 363-374, October 1961.
McCafferty, J.A. *The death sentence, 1960. In* The death penalty in American ; an anthology. Edited by H.A. Bedau. Garden City, N.Y., Anchor Books, 1964, p. 90-103.
McCafferty, J.A. *Major trends in the use of capital punishment.* Federal Probation. Washington, D.C., 25 : 15-21, September 1961.
McCafferty, J.A. *Trends in capital punishment. In* Proceedings of the 97th Annual Congress of Correction. Washington, D.C., American Correctional Association, 1967, p. 23-27.
McCall, D.J. *Evolution of capital punishment in Wyoming : a reconciliation of social retribution and humane concern ?* Land and Water Law Review. Laramie, WY, 13 : 865-907, 1978, no. 3.
McClean, J.D. and Wood, J.C. *Obsolete penalties. In* Criminal justice and the treatment of offenders. London, Sweet and Maxwell, 1969, p. 282-297.
McClellan, G.S. ed. *Capital punishment.* New York, N.Y., H.W. Wilson Company, 1961, 180 p.
McDaniel JR., W.A. Gardner v. Florida : *the application of due process to sentencing procedures.* Virginia Law Review. Charlottesville, VA, 63 : 1281-1298, 1977, no. 7.
McDonald, L. *Capital punishment in South Carolina : the end of an era.* South Carolina Law Review. Columbia, S.C., 24 : 762, 1972.
McFadden, G.T. *Capital sentencing :* effect of McGautha and Furman. Temple Law Quarterly. Philadelphia, PA, 45 : 619-648, 1972.
McFarland, S.G. *Is capital punishment a short-term deterrent to homicide ? A study of the effects of four recent American executions.* Journal of Criminal Law and Criminology. Chicago, IL, 74 : 1014-1032, 1983, no. 3.
McGahey, R.M. *Dr. Erhlich's magic bullet : economic theory, econometrics, and the death penalty.* Crime and Delinquency. Hackensack, N.J., 26 : 485-502, 1980, no. 4.
McGee, R.A. *Capital punishment as seen by a correctional administrator.* Federal Probation. Washington, D.C., 28 : 11-16, June 1964.
McGehee, E.G. and Hildebrand, W.H. eds. *The death penalty : a literary and historical approach.* Boston, MA, D.C. Heath and Co., 1964.
McGrath, W.T. *Should Canada abolish the gallows and the lash ?* Winnipeg, Man., Stovel Advocate Press, 1956, 95 p.
McIntyre, D.M. *Delays in the execution of death sentences.* Chicago, IL, American Bar Association, 1960.
McKee, D.L. and Sesnowitz, M.L. *Welfare economic aspects of capital*

punishment. American Journal of Economics and Sociology. Dunedin, FL, 35 : 41-47, 1976.
Mackey, P.E. *Edward Livingston on the punishment of death.* Tulane Law Review. New Orleans, LA, 48 : 25-42, December 1973.
Mackey, P.E. *Hanging in the balance : the anti-capital punishment movement in New York State, 1776-1861.* New York, N.Y., Garland, 1982, 355 p.
Mackey, P.E. *The inutility of mandatory capital punishment : an historical note.* Boston University Law Review. Boston, MA, 54 : 32-35, January 1974, no. 1. Also in Capital punishment in the United States. Edited by H. Bedau and C. M. Pierce. New York, N.Y., AMS Press, 1976.
Mackey, P.E. ed. *Voices against death : American opposition to capital punishment, 1787-1975.* New York, N.Y., Burt Franklin, 1976.
Mackey, P.E. ed. *Voices against death : classic appeals against the death penalty in America, 1787-1975.* New York, N.Y., Burt Franklin, 1976.
McLean, R. *Reconstruction of Arizona's death penalty statute under* Watson. Arizona Law Review. Tucson, AZ, 22 : 1037-1053, 1980, no. 4.
McManus, W.S. *Estimates of the deterrent effect of capital punishment : the importance of the research's prior beliefs.* Journal of Political Economy. Chicago, IL, 93 : 417-425, 1985, no. 2.
MacNamara, D.E.J. *Convicting the innocent.* Crime and Delinquency. Hackensack, N.J., 15 : 57-62, January 1969.
MacNamara, D.E.J. *Statement against capital punishment. In* The death penalty in America ; an anthology. Edited by H.A. Bedau. Garden City, N.Y., Anchor Books, 1964, p. 182-192.
MacNamara, D.E.J., *A survey of recent literature on capital punishment.* American Journal of Correction. St. Paul, MN, 24 : 16/19, March-April 1962.
McNeil, G. and Vance S. *Cruel and unusual.* Ottawa, Ont., 1978, 179 p.
Macrae, A.K.M. *An irrelevant penalty. In* The hanging question. Edited by L. Blom-Cooper. London, Duckworth and CO., 1969, p. 105-108.
Maas, M.P. *Halsgericht (Name of a German Medieval court).* Darmstadt, Siegfried Toeche-Mittler Verlag, 1968, 288 p.
Macior, W. *Kara smierci jako ultima ratio (The death penalty as the last resort).* Panstwo i Prawo. Warsaw, no. 9-12 : 91-95, 1981.
Maddox, J. *An indecent ritual. In* The hanging question. Edited by L. Blom-Cooper. London, Duckworth and Co., 1969, p. 83-90.
Maeda, T. *(Decreasing tendency of capital punishment in Japan).* Acta Criminologiae et Medicinae Legalis Japonica. Tokyo, 39 : 29-36, June 1973. In Japanese.
Maeda, T. *How will the number of capital punishments decrease in Japan ?* Acta Criminologiae et Medicinae Legalis Japonica. Tokyo, 43 : 47-48, June 1977.
Maes, L.T. *La peine de mort dans le droit criminel de Malines (Capital punishment in Malines criminal law).* Revue Historique de Droit Français et Etranger. Paris : 379, 1950.
Mahee, D. *Slow coming dark :* interviews on death row. New York, N.Y., The Pilgrim Press, 1980.
Mailer, N. *The executioner's song.* Boston, MA, Little, Brown, 1979.
Maines, R. *The death penalty for juveniles : a constitutional alternative.*

Journal of Juvenile Law. La Verne, CA, 7 : 54-67, 1983.
Malenkovsky, J. *Trešt śmrti v soucasńem miezinarodnim spolecentstvi (The death penalty in the contemporary international community).* Parvny Obzor. Bratislawa, no. 4 : 370-379, 1984.
Malo Camacho, G. *Hacia la abolición de la pena de muerte en México (Towards the abolition of the death penalty in Mexico).* Revista Mexicana de Prevención y Readaptación Social. México, D.F., 2 : 11-19, octubre-diciembre 1974.
Manas Ruiz, J. *La pena de muerte a la luz de la doctrine de Juan Luns Escoto (The death penalty according to Juan Duns Escoto).* Revista de la Escuela de Estudios Penitenciarios. Madrid : 49-56, septoembre-octubre 1965.
Mannheim, H. *Capital punishment : what next ?* Fortnightly Review (now Contemporary Review. London : 213-221, October 1948.
Mannheim, K.M. *The capital punishment cases : a criticism of judicial methods.* Loyola of Los Angeles Law Review. Los Angeles, CA, 12 : 85-134, 1978, no. 1.
Manrique Zermeno, E. *Respuesta al cuestionario de Naciones Unidas sobre la pena de muerte en México (Answers to the UN questionnaire on capital punishment in Mexico).* Derecho Penal Contemporaneo. Mexico, D.F., no. 15 : 55-81, julio-agosto 1966.
Marcotte, M. *Libération de l'homme et respect de la vie (Man's liberation and respect for life).* Relations, Montréal, Que., no. 360 : 132, mai 1971.
Marcus, M. and Weissbrodt, D.S. *The death penalty cases.* California Law Review. Berkeley, CA, 56 : 1270-1490, October 1968.
Mark, R. *The aftermath of hanging.* Security Gazette. London, 23 : 11, 1980, no. 1.
Marshall, T. *Remarks on the death penalty made at the Judicial Conference of the Second Circuit.* Columbia Law Review. Urvington, N.Y., 86 : 1-8, 1986, no. 1.
Marti, J. *Por qué la pena de muerte ? (Why capital punishment ?)* Enquiridion. Havana : 3-7, abril-junio 1956.
Martin, J.B. *Crime of passion. In* The death penalty in American ; an anthology. Edited by H.A. Bedau. Garden City, N.Y., Anchor Books, 1964.
Martin, J.B. *The question of identity. In* The death penalty in America ; an anthology. Edited by H.A. Bedau, p. 439-548.
Marx, K. *Smrtna kazna (The death penalty).* In Dela Vol. 11. By K. Marx and F. Engels. Beograd, 1975, p. 419-424.
Marx, K. and Engels, F. *Die Todesstrafe (The death penalty).* In Werke. Berlin, GDR, 1960, p. 506-513.
Mastro Titta. *Il boia di Roma ; memorie de un carnefice scritte da lui stesso (Rome's hangman ; an executioner's memoirs written by himself).* Roma, Arcana Editrice, 1971, 332 p.
Matter of life and death – due process protection in capital clemency proceedings. Yale Law Journal. New Haven, CT, 90 : 889-911, 1981, no. 4.
Mattick, H.W. *The unexamined death ; an analysis of capital punishment.* 2nd ed. Chicago, IL. John Howard Association, 1966, 46 p.
Maurach, R. *Todesstrafe in der Sowjetunion (The death penalty in the Soviet Union).* Osteuropa. Stuttgart, no. 11/12 : 751, 1963.

Maxwell Fyfe, D. *The death penalty.* Revue Internationale de Droit Pénal. Pau, 19 : 135-144, 1948.

Meador, R. *Capital revenge : 54 votes against life.* Philadelphia, PA, Dorrance and Co. Inc., 1975, 322 p.

Meiners, R.G. *Justice or revenge ?* Dickinson Law Review. Carlisle, PA, 60 : 342-347, June 1956.

Mello, M. *Florida « heinous, atrocious and cruel » aggravating circumstance : narrowing the class of death-eligible cases without making it smaller.* Stetson Law Review. DeLand, FL, 13 : 523-554, 1984.

Mello, M. and Robson R. *Judge over jury : Florida's practice of imposing death over life in capital cases.* Florida State University Law Review. Tallahassee, FL, 13 : 31-75, 1985.

Meltsner, M. *Cruel and unusual ; the Supreme Court and capital punishment.* New York, N.Y., William Morrow and Co. Inc., 1973, 338 p.

Meltsner, M. *Litigating against the death penalty :* the strategy behing Furman. Yale Law Journal. New Haven, CT, 82 : 1111, May 1973.

Meneu Monleon, P. *Los abogados argentinos contra la pena de muerte (Argentinian lawyers against capital punishment).* Anuario de Derecho Penal y Ciencias Penales. Madrid, 23 : 655-658, septiembre-diciembre 1970.

Meneu Monleon, P. *No a la pena de muerte en Espana (No to the death penalty in Spain).* In Aktuelle kriminologie. Hamburg, Kriminalistick Verlag, 1969, p. 25-29.

Menninger, K. *The crime of punishment.* New York, N.Y., Viking Press, 1969, 305 p.

Meinninger, K. *Verdict guilty : now what ? In* A psychiatrist's world : the selected papers of Karl Menninger. Edited by Hall., New York, N.Y., Viking Press, 1959.

Mental suffering under sentence of death : a cruel and unusual punishment. Iowa Law Review. Iowa City, IA, 57 : 814, February 1972.

Mereu, I. *La morte come pena (Death as punishment).* Milano, Editori Europei Associati, 1982, 182 p.

Metropolitan Life Insurance Company. Punishment for murder. Statistical Bulletin. New York, N.Y., 33 : 4-6, February 1952.

Mewshaw, M. *Life for death.* Garden City, N.Y., Doubleday, 1980, 281 p.

Meyer, H.H.B. *Select list of references on capital punishment.* Washington, D.C., Government Printing Office, 1912.

Middendorff, W. *Dr. Dodd and the death penalty for forgery : an essay in historical criminology.* Crime, Punishment and Correction. Cape Town, 3 : 88-93, February 1974.

Middendorff, W. *Todesstrafe : ja oder nein ? (The death penalty : yes or no ?)* Freiburg i Br., Rombach, 1961, 80 p.

Midgley, J. *Public opinion and the death penalty in South Africa.* British Journal of Criminology. London, 14 : 345-358, 1974, 4.

Miklau, R. *The death penalty : a decisive question.* Crime Prevention and Criminal Justice Newsletter. Vienna, no. 12/13 : 39-42, November 1986.

Milenkovic, S. *Abolition of the death penalty : deliberations at the United Nations.* Review of International Affairs. Belgrade, 37 : 15-18, 2 March 1986.

Milic, M. *Dva krivicnopravna akta ujedinjenih nacija i njihov domasaj (Two legal UN instruments and their effects).* Nasa Zakonitostz. Zagreb, 24 : 460-475, 1975.
Mill, J.S. *Remarks on capital punishment within Prisons Bill.* Westminster Review. London, 91 : 429-436, April 1869.
Miller, A.V. *Capital punishment as a deterrent : a bibliography.* Monticello, IL, Vance Bibliographies, 1980, 11 p. and supplement 23 p.
Miller, D. ed. *Death penalty update.* Des Moines, IA, Iowa Edition, 121 p.
Milligan, C.S. *A protestant's view of the death penalty. In* The death penalty in America ; an anthology. Edited by H.A. Bedau. Garden City, N.Y., Anchor Books, 1964, p. 175-182.
Millman, F. *Financing the right to counsel in death penalty cases.* Loyola of Los Angeles Law Review. Los Angeles, CA, 19 : 383-390, 1985.
Milton, F. *More than a crime : studies in murder by legal process.* London, Pall Mall, 1962, 252 p.
Mironenko, Y.P. *The re-emergence of the death penalty in the Soviet Union.* Soviet Affairs Analysis Service. Münich, no. 28 : 1-5, 1961-1962.
Mittermaier, C.J.A. *De la peine de mort (On capital punishment).* Paris, Sirey, 1865.
Miyazawa, K. *(Social conditions underlying the abolition of capital punishment with reference to West Germany and Italy).* Hôritsu Jiho. Japan, 42 : 8, May 1970. In Japanese.
Moberly, W. *Capital punishment.* Howard Journal. Chichester, 9, 1954, no. 1.
Moberly, W. *The ethics of punishment.* London, Faber and Faber, 1968.
Mode of capital punishment. Social Defence. New Delhi, 7 : 50-51, April 1972.
Moore, M. *Attitude toward capital punishment : scale validation.* Psychological Reports. Missoula, MT, 37 : 21-22, 1975, no. 1.
Moraes, B. *A evoluçao do pensemento anglo-americano sobre a pena de morte (The evolution of Anglo-American thought on capital punishment).* Revista Brasileira de Criminologia e Direito Penal. Rio de Janeiro, no. 6 : 87-98, julio-septiembre 1964.
Moran, G. and Comfort, J.C. *Neither « tentative » nor « fragmentary » : verdict preference of impaneled felony jurors as a function of attitude toward capital punishment.* Journal of Applied Psychology. Washington, D.C., 71 : 146-155, 1986, no. 1.
Morón Alcaín, E. *Pena de muerte poder del estado y supresión de la vida segun el derecho natural (Capital punishment, power of the state and suppression of life according to natural law).* Panorama Criminológico. Cordoba : 13-15, noviembre 1979.
Morris, A. *Thoughts on capital punishment.* Washington Law Review. Seattle, WA, 35 : 335-361, Fall 1960.
Morris, N. *Hans Mattick and the death penalty : sentimental notes on two topics.* University of Toledo Law Review. Toledo, OH, 10 : 299-316, 1979, no. 2.
Morris, N. and Hawkins, G. *The honest politician's guide to crime control.* Chicago, IL, University of Chicago Press, 1970, 271 p.
Morrison, W.A. *Criminal homicide and the death penalty in Canada : time*

for re-assessment and new directions : toward a typology of homicide. Canadian Journal of Criminology and Corrections. Ottawa, Ont., 15 : 367-396, 1973, no. 4.

Morsbach, H. and Morsbach, G. *Attitudes towards capital punishment in South Africa.* British Journal of Criminology. London : 394-403, 1967.

Mulligan, W.H. *Cruel and unusual punishment : the proportionality rule.* Fordham Law Review. New York, N.Y., 47 : 639-650, 1979, no. 5.

Mullin, C. *Jury system in death penalty cases : a symbolic gesture.* Law and Contemporary Problems. Durham, N.C., 43 : 137-154, 1980, no. 4.

Mungenast, E.M. *Der Moerder und der Stast. Die Todesstrafe im Urteil hervorragender Zeitgenossen (Murder and the state. The death penalty as viewed by important contemporary writers).* Stuttgart, 1928, 92 p.

Munoz Pope, C. *La pena capital en Centroamérica (Capital punishment in Central America).* Panama. Panama Viejo, 1978.

Munteanu, R. *La notion de droit à la vie dans les conventions universelles (The notion of the right to life in world conventions).* Sciences Juridiques, 29 : 33-51, 1985.

Murder and capital punishment in England and Wales. London, National Campaign for the Abolition of Capital Punishment and the Howard League for Penal Reform, 1974, 17 p.

Murdy, R.G. *A moderate view of capital punishment.* Federal Probation. Washington, D.C., 25 : 11-15, September 1961.

Murphy, J.W. *Technology, humanism, and death by injection.* Philosophy and Social Action. New Delhi, 11 : 55-63, October-December 1985.

Murton, T. *Treatment of condemned prisoners.* Crime and Delinquency. Hackensack, N.J., 15 : 94, 1969.

Musman, J.L. *Death penalty as cruel and unusual punishment for rape.* William and Mary Law Review. Williamsburg, VA, 12 : 682, Spring 1971.

Myers, G.E. *The death penalty.* Criminal Justice Review, Atlanta, GA, 6 : 48-53, 1981, no. 1.

Nakell, B. and Hardy, K.A. *The arbitrariness of death penalty.* Philadelphia, PA, Temple University Press, 1987.

Nakell, B. *The cost of the death penalty.* Criminal Law Bulletin. Boston, MA, 14 : 69-80, 1978, no. 1. Also in The death penalty in America. Edited by H.A. Bedau, 3rd ed. Oxford. Oxford University Press, 1982, p. 241-246.

Nathanson, S. *Does it matter if the death penalty is arbitrarily administered ?* Philosophy and Public Affairs. Princeton, N.J., 14 : 149-164, 1985, no. 2.

National Council on Crime and Delinquency. Capital punishment. Crime and Delinquency. Hackensack, N.J., 15, January 1969. Special issue.

National Council Board of Trustees. Policy statement on capital punishment. Crime and Delinquency. Hackensack, N.J., 10 : 105-109, April 1964.

National Council NCCD submits brief in death penalty case. Federal Probation. Washington, D.C., 34 : 84, June 1970.

National Interreligious Task Force on Criminal Justice. Work Group on the Death Penalty. Capital punishment : what the religious community says. New York, N.Y., 1978, 39 p.

Naud, A. *Tu ne tueras pas (You shall not kill).* Paris, Morgan, 1959.

Neapolitan, J. *Support for and opposition to capital punishment.* Criminal Justice and Behavior. Beverly Hills, CA, 10 : 195-208, 1983, no. 2.
Nesbitt, C.A. *Managing death row.* Corrections Today. College Park, MD, 48 : 90-95, 1986, no. 5.
Neser, J. *To hang or not to hang, that is the question.* South African Journal of Criminal Law and Criminology. Linetown, 10 : 129-134, 1986, no. 2.
Neustatter, W.L. *The mind of the murderer.* New York, N.Y., Philosophical Library, 1957.
Nevares-Muniz, D. The eighth amendment revisited : a model of weighted punishments. Journal of Criminal Law and Criminology. Chicago, IL, 75 : 272-289, 1984, no. 1.
Neves de Alencar, A. *Ayres Valdarez. Pena de morte (Capital punishment).* Revista de Informaçao Legislative. Brasilia, 8 : 121, jan-marzo 1971.
New Illinois death penalty : double constitutional trouble. Loyola University Law Journal. Chicago, IL, 5 : 351-393, Summer 1974.
New York state Defenders Association. Capital cases : the price of the death penalty for New York State. Albany, N.Y., NYSPDA, 1982.
Newman, G.R. *The punishment response.* Philadelphia, PA, Lippincott, 1977, 323 p.
Nietzel, M.T. and Dillehay, R.C. *The effects of variations in voire dire procedures in capital murder trials.* Law and Human Behavior. New York, N.Y., 6 : 1-13, 1982, no. 1.
Nishikawa, T. *Capital punishment in Japan.* Paper presented at the Interdisciplinary Conference on Capital Punishment, April 1980. Atlanta, GA, Georgia State University.
Normand, M. *La peine de mort (Capital punishment).* Paris, Presses Universitaires de France, 1980, 127 p.
Normandeau, A. *La peine de mort au Canada (Capital punishment in Canada).* Revue de Droit Pénal et de Criminologie, Bruxelles, 46 : 547-560, 1965-1966.
Normandeau, A. *Peine de mort, peine perdue ! (Capital punishment, lost punishment !)* Maintenant, Montréal, Que. : 238-243, juillet-août 1965.
Normandeau, A. *Pioneers in criminology : Charles Lucas : opponent of capital punishment.* Journal of Criminal Law, Criminology and Police Science. Baltimore, MD, 61 : 218-228, June 1970.
Norris, W. *One from seven-hundred.* New York, N.Y., Pergamon Press, 1966.
Novotny, O. *Trest smrti a platne trestni pravo (The death penalty as a penal sanction).* Pravnik. Prague, no. 6 : 524, 1967.
Nsereko, D.D. and Glickman, M.J.A. *Capital punishment in Botswana.* Crime Prevention and Criminal Justice Newsletter. Vienna, no. 12/13 : 51-53, November 1986.
Nuvolone, P. *La pena di morte (Capital Punishment).* Indice Penale. Prodova, 9 : 453-455, settembre-dicembre 1975.
Oberer, W.E. *Does disqualification of jurors for scruples against capital punishment constitue denial of fair trial on issue of guilt ?* Texas Law Review, Austin, TX, 39 : 545-567, May 1961.
Oerton, R.T. *L'abolition de la peine de mort en Grande-Bretagne (The abo-*

lition of capital punishment in Great Britain). Revue de Science Criminelle et de Droit Pénal Comparé. Paris : 147-148, 1966.
Olivecrona, K. D'. *De la peine de mort (On the death penalty).* 2nd ed. Translated by Beauchet, Paris, Arthur Rousseau, 1893.
Olmesdahl, M.C.J. *Predicting the death sentence.* South African Journal of Criminal Law and Criminology. Durban, no. 3 : 201-218, 1982.
Olmstead, J. *The constitutional right to assistance in addition to counsel in a death penalty case.* Duquesne Law Review. Pittsburgh, PA, 23 : 753-772, 1985.
Onder, A. *Olum cezasi (The death penalty).* Ankara Barosu Dergisi. Ankara, 18 : 1-6, 1961, no. 1.
Orelli, A. *La peine de mort en Suisse ((The death penalty in Switzerland).* Revue de Droit International et de Législation Comparée. Brussels. 11 : 382, 1879.
Organization of American States. Inter-American Commission on Human Rights. Resolution, no. 3/87, Case no.
Orton, M.W. *Constitutional law : State statute allowing jury discretion in imposing the death sentence which is not arbitrary and capricious does not violate the eighth and fourteenth amendments.* Jurek v. Texas. Howard Law Journal. Washington, D.C., 20 : 500-511, 1977, no. 2.
Ortved, W.N. *Reform of the law relating to capital punishment : a study in the operation of parliamentary institutions.* Faculty of Law Review. Toronto, Ont., 29 : 73, August 1971.
Oshman, R. *An impermissible punishment : the decline of consistency as a constitutional goal in capital sentencing.* Place Law Review. Brooklyn, NY, 5 : 371-402, 1985.
Paget, R.T., Silverman, S. and Hollis, C. *Hanged : and innocent ?* London, Victor Gollancz Ltd., 1953.
Paine, D.F. *Capital punishment.* Tennessee Law Review. Knoxville, TN, 29 : 534-552, Summer 1962.
Palacios y Andrade, A.E. *La pena de muerte como solución al problema de la delinquencia en México (The death penalty as a solution to the problem of delinquency in Mexico).* México, D.F., Escuela Libre de Derecho, 1973, 170 p.
Palazzo, F.C. *Pena di morte e diritti umani (a proposito del Sesto protocollo addizionale alla Convenzione europea dei diritti dell'uomo (The death penalty and human rights : with regard to the 6th Additional Protocol to the European Convention on Human Rights).* Rivista Italiana di Diritto e Procedura Penale. Milano, 27 : 759-774, 1984, no. 2.
Palmer, L.I. *Two perspectives on structuring discretion : Justices Stewart and White on the death penalty.* Journal of Criminal Law and Criminology. Baltimore, MD, 70 : 194-213, 1979, no. 2.
Palomba, I. *Devianza minorile e pena di morte (Juvenile delinquency and capital punishment).* Quaderni della Giustizia. Roma, 6 : 89-93, Ottobre 1986.
Panick, D. *Judicial review of the death penalty.* London, Duckworth, 1982, 245 p.
Parada, N. *La pena capital y su ineficacia en la profilaxis del delito (The death penalty and its uselessness as a deterrent against crime).* Revista de

Criminologia y Ciencias Penales. La Paz, no. 5 : 55-57, 1947.
Parker II, R.A. The current status of the death penalty in North Carolina. Wake Forest Law Review. Winston-Salem, N.C., 9 : 135-141, December 1972.
Parnass, G. *The disinterment of an ancient law an eye for an eye, no death for rape.* Brooklyn Law Review. Brooklyn, N.Y., 44 : 622-636, 1978, no. 3.
Partington, D. *The incidence of the death penalty for rape in Virginia.* Washington and Lee Law Review. Lexington, VA, 22 : 43-73, 1965.
Pascucci, R. *Capital punishment in 1984 : abandoning the pursuit of firness and consistency. Cornell Law Review. Ithaca, N.Y., 69 : 1129-1243, 1984.*
Passell, P. and Taylor, J.B. The deterrence controversy : a reconsideration of the time series evidence. In Capital punishment in the United States. Edited by H.A. Bedau and C.M. Pierce. New York, N.Y., AMS Press, 1976, p. 359-371.
Passell, P. *The deterrent effect of the death penalty : a statistical test.* Stanford Law Review. Stanford, CA, 28 : 61-80, November 1975. Also in Capital punishment in the United States. Edited by H.A. Bedau and C.M. Pierce, New York, N.Y., AMS Press, 1976, p. 396-416.
Paternoster, R. *Prosecutorial discretion in requesting the death penalty : a case of victim-based racial discrimination.* Law and Society Review. Denver, CO, 18 : 437-478, 1984, no. 3.
Paternoster, R. *Race of victim and location of crime : the decision to seek the death penalty in South Carolina.* Journal of Criminal Law and Criminology. Chicago, IL, 74 : 754-785, 1983, no. 3.
Paton, J. *The abolition debate.* Penal Reformer. Loncon, 5, January 1939.
Paton, J. *Abolition in parliament.* Penal Reformer. London, 6, July 1939.
Paton, J. *Democracy and the death penalty.* Penal Reformer. London, 2, July 1935.
Paton, J. *Justice is blindfolded.* Penal Reformer. London, 5, July 1938.
Paton, J. *An open letter to the Lord Chief Justice.* Penal Reformer. London, 2, January 1936.
Patrick, C.H. *The status of capital punishment : a world perspective.* Journal of Criminal Law, Criminology and Police Science. Baltimore, MD, 56 : 397-411, December 1965.
Pearson, B.L. ed. *The death penalty in South Carolina : outlook for the 1980s.* Columbia, S.C., Aclusc Press, 1981, 167 p.
Peck, J.K. *The deterrent effect of capital punishment : Ehrlich and nis critics.* Yale Law Journal. New Haven, CT, 85 : 359-367, 1976, no. 3.
Pedregal, L.J. *Los tormentos en la historia y la pena de decapitación (Torture in history and beheading).* Revista de la Escuela de Estudios Penitenciarios. Madrid : 100-106, 1955.
La peine capitale (Capital punishment). International Review of Criminal Policy. New York, N.Y. : 130-139 and 146-155, January 1954.
Peine capitale (Capital punishment). Réadaptation. Ottawa, Ont., 11 : 2, avril 1970.
La peine de mort (Capital punishment). By M. Muller and others. Archives de l'Institut de Médecine Légale et de Médecine Sociale de Lille. Lille : 45-77, 1966.
La peine de mort devant la chambre française (Capital punishment in the

French Parliament). Revue de Droit Pénal et de Criminologie. Bruxelles : 281-286, 1909.

Pena de Morte. Coloquio Internacional Comemorativo do Centenario da Aboliçao da Pena de Morte em Portugal (The death penalty. A comemorative symposium on the centennial of the abolition of capital punishment in Portugal). Coimbra, Faculdade de Direito, Universidade de Coimbra, 1967, 3 vols.

La Pena de muerte – 6 respuestas (The death penalty : 6 answers). By M. Barbero Santos and others. Valladolid, Universidad de Valladolid, Departemento de Derecho Penal, 1975, 218 p.

La Pena di morte abolita negli Stati Uniti d'America (The death penalty abolished in the United States). Scuola Positiva. Milano, 14 : 442, 1972, no. 3.

Pena di morte e pensiero cattolico (The death penalty and catholic thought). Scuola Positiva. Milano, 4 : 306-307, 1972, no. 2.

The Penalty for murder. Justice of the Peace. Chichester, 138 : 673-675, December 1974.

Pennell, L.T. *Capital punishment.* Alberta Law Review. Edmonton, Alta., 5 : 167-174, 1967, no. 2.

Pennsylvania ruling bans death penalty. Federal Probation. Washington, D.C., 35 : 76, March 1971.

People under sentence of death as of August 4, 1971. New York, N.Y., Citazns against Legal Murder Inc., 1971.

Perrault, G. Le pull-over rouge (The red pull-over). Paris, Editions Ramsay, 1978, 432 p.

Pesic, V. *Ubistva u Jugoslaviji (Homicide in Yugoslavia).* Beograd, IKSKI, 1972.

Petersen, D.M. and Truzzi M. eds. *Criminal life : views from the inside.* Englewood Cliffs, N.J., Prentice Hall International, 1972, 228 p.

Phelps, H.A. *Rhode Island's threat against murder.* Journal of Criminal Law, Criminology and Police Science. Baltimore, MD, 18 : 552-567, February, 1928.

Phillips, D.P. *Deterrence and the death penalty : reply to Zeisel.* American Journal of Sociology. Chicago, IL, 88 : 170-172, 1982, no. 1.

Phillips, D.P. *The deterrent effect of capital punishment : new evidence on an old controversy.* American Journal of Sociology. Chicago, IL, 86 : 139-148, 1980, no. 1.

Phillips, D.P. *The fluctuation of homicides after publicized executions : reply to Kobbervig, Inverarity, and Lauderdale.* American Journal of Sociology. Chicago, IL, 88 : 165-167, 1982, no. 1.

Piedelièvre, R. *Le problème de la peine de mort (The problem of capital punishment).* Bulletin de la Société Internationale de Criminologie. Paris : 28-34, 1er et 2e semestres, 1953.

Pierrepoint, A. *Executioner :* Pierrepoint, an autobiography. London, George G. Harrap and Co. Ltd., 1974, 211 p.

Pilat, T. *W kwestii kary śmierci (On the question of the death penalty).* Problemy Praworzadności, no. 8-9 : 46-56, 1986.

Plawski, S. *L'abolition de la peine de mort (The abolition of the death penalty).* Revue Pénitentiaire et de Droit Pénal. Paris : 473-476, octobre-decembre 1981.

Plawski, S. *La peine de mort (The death penalty).* Revue Pénitentiaire et de Droit Pénal. Paris : 257-262, avril-juin 1973.

Playfair, G. and Sington, D. *The offenders : the case against legal vengeance.* New York, N.Y., Simon and Schuster, 1957.

Pleas of the condemned : should certiorari petitions from death row receive enhanced access to the Supreme Court ? New York University Law Review. New York, N.Y., 59 : 1120-1149, 1984.

Poe, D.A. *Capital punishment statutes in the wake of* United States v. Jackson : some unresolved questions. George Washington University Law Review. Washington, D.C., 37 : 719-745, May 1969.

Poenaru, I. *Contributii la studiul pedepssei capital (Contribution to the study of capital punishment).* Bucuresti, 1974, 254 p.

Poenaru, I. *Zur Frage der Todesstrafe (On the question of capital punishment).* Jahrbuch fuer Ostrecht. Stuttgart, XV : 195-198, 1 und 2 Halbjahresheft, 1974.

Poklewski-Koziell, K. *Refleksja o « Refleksjach o karze śmierci w swietle teorii penalnych (Comments on « Reflections on the death penalty in the light of penal theories »).* Nowe Prawo. Warsaw, no. 10 : 98-101, 1986.

Polianskij, N.N. *Proval zakonoproekta ob ogranichenii sprimenenia smertnoi kazni v Anglii (Comment on the draft law regarding limited application of the death penalty in England).* Sovetskoe Gosudarstvo i Pravo. Moscow, no. 929, 1948.

Polsby, D.D. *The death of capital punishment ?* Furman v. Georgia. Supreme Court Review. Chicago, IL : 1-40, 1972.

Poncet, D. *Vers l'abolition de la peine de mort en Angleterre (Towards the abolition of capital punishment in England).* Revue Internationale de Criminologie et Police Technique. Genève, 10 : 60-62, janvier-mars 1956.

Portugal. *Directorate General of Information. Death penalty ? We have abolished it in 1867.* Bulletin of the Directorate General of Information. Lisbon, March 1971, no. 9.

Potas, I. and Walker, J. *Capital punishment.* Woden, A.C.T., Australian Institute of Criminology, 1987, 6 p.

Potter, J.D. *The art of hanging.* Cranbury, N.J., Barnes and Co. Inc., 1971, 196 p.

Powell, R.L. *Capital punishment.* Georgia Journal of Corrections. Atlanta, GA, 3 : 8, August 1974.

Powers, E. *The legal history of capital punishment in Massachusetts.* Federal Probation. Washington, D.C., 45 : 15-20, 1981, no. 3.

Prettyman Jr, B. *Death and the Supreme Court.* New York, N.Y., Harcourt, Brace and World Inc., 1961, 311 p.

Príchystal, V. *Zruśime trest smrti (Changing the death penalty).* Socialistická Zákonnost. Prague, no. 7 : 389, 1969.

Primorac, I. *On Capital punishment.* Israel Law Review. Jerusalem, 17 : 133-150, 1982, no. 2.

Primorac, I. *Prestud i kazna (Deviance and punishment).* Beograd, Mladost, 1978.

Pritchard, J.L. *A history of capital punishment.* New York, N.Y., 1960, 230 p.
Problem smrtne kazne u nas danas (Problems of the death penalty today). Nasa Zakonitestz. Zagreb, no. 2 : 137-182, 1974.
Le problème de la peine capitale : systématisation des réponses au questionnaire des Nations Unies (The problem of capital punishment : structuring the answers to the UN questionnaire). Annales Internationales de Criminologie. Paris, 472-517, juillet-décembre 1983.
Le problème de la peine de mort (The problem of capital punishment). Bulletin de la Société Internationale de Criminologie. Paris : 11-62, 1953.
Prokosch, E. *La pena di morte nel mondo (The death penalty in the world). In* La pena di morte nel mondo. By Amnesty International. Casale Monferrato, Marietti, 1963, p. 1-12.
Psychiatrists and execution. Psychiatric News. Washington, D.C., 16 : 22, 1981, no. 12.
Psychiatrists urged to fight use of hypothetical questions in court on defendants mental state. Psychiatric News. Washington, D.C.), D.C., 18 : 3, 1983, n° 24.
Pugsley, R. *Retributive arguments against capital punishment.* Hofstra Law Review. Hampstead, N.Y., 9 : 1501-1523, 1981.
Quade, V. *Cheaper to kill ? ABA eyes the death penalty.* American Bar Association Journal. Chicago, IL, 71 : 17, April 1983.
Quanter, R. Die Leibes – und Lebensstrafen bei allen Voelkern und zu allen Zeiten (Corporal and capital punishment amongst all peoples and at all times). Aalen, 1970, 476 p.
La question de la peine de mort (The question of the death penalty). Revue de Droit Pénal et de Criminologie. Bruxelles : 63, 1907 ; 281-288, 1909 ; 887, 1910.
The Question of capital punishment. By S. Nicolai and others. Lincoln, NE, Contact Inc., 1980, 152 p.
Quillin, W.C. *The death penalty in the Soviet Union.* American Journal of Criminal Law. Austin, TX, 5 : 225-246, 1977, no. 2.
Quiroz Cuaron, A. *La pena de muerte en Mexico (The death penalty in Mexico).* Mexico, D.F. Ediciones Botas, 1962, 103 p.
Rabbikin, J. *Justice and judicial hand writing : the death penalty since.* Gregg. Criminal Justice Ethics. New York, N.Y., 4 : 18-29, 1985.
Radelet, M.L. ed. *Death row confinement.* Special issue of Death Studies. New York, N.Y., 1987.
Radelet, M.L. and Bernard, G. *Ethics and the psychiatric determination of competency to be executed.* Bulletin of the American Academy of Psychiatric and Law. Pittsburgh, PA, 14 : 37-53, 1986.
Radelet, M.L. and Mello, M. *Executing those kill blacks : an « Unusual case » study.* Mercer University Law Review. Macon, GA, 37 : 911-925, 1985.
Radelet, M.L., Vandiver, M. and Berardo, F. *Families, prisons, and men with death sentences.* Journal of Family Issues. Beverly Hills, Ca, 4 : 593-612, 1983.
Radelet, M.L., Vandiver, M. and Berardo, F. *The Florida Supreme Court*

and death penalty appeals. Journal of Criminal Law and Criminology. Chicago, IL, 74 : 913-926, 1983, n° 3.
Radelet, M.L., Vandiver, M. and Berardo, F. *Race and capital punishment : an overview of the issues.* Crime and Social Justice. San Francisco, CA, 1986.
Radelet, M.L. and Pierce, G.L. *Race and prosecutorial discretion in homicide cases.* Law and Society Review. Denver, CO, 19 : 587-621, 1985.
Radelet, M.L. *Racial characteristics and imposition of the death penalty.* American Sociological Review. Albany, N.Y., 46 : 918-927, 1981, no. 6.
Radelet, M.L. *Rejecting the jury : the imposition of the death penalty in Florida.* University of California Davis Law Review. Davis, CA, 18 : 1409-1431, 1985.
Rader, J.N. *Capital punishment – Rape – Death held to be a cruel and unusual punishment for the crime of rape of an adult woman.* Coker v. Georgia, 97 S. Ct. 2861 (1977). American Journal of Criminal Law. Austin, TX, 6 : 107-118, 1978, no. 1.
Radin, M.J. *Cruel punishment and respect for persons : super due process for death.* Southern California Law Review. Los Angeles, CA, 53 : 1143-1185, 1980, no. 4.
Radin, M.J. *Jurisprudence of death : evolving standards for the cruel and unusual punishments clause.* University of Pennsylvania Law Review. Philadelphia, PA, 126 : 989-1064, 1978, no. 5.
Radin, M.J. *Proportionality, subjectivity, and tragedy.* University of California Davis Law Review. Davis, CA, 18 : 1165-1176, 1985.
Radzinowicz, L. *Changing attitudes towards crime and punishment.* Law Quarterly Review. Agincourt. Ont., 75, 1959.
Radzinowicz, L. *A history of English criminal law and its administration from 1750.* Vol. 1, London, Stevens, 1948.
Rahav, G. *The deterrence effect of the death penalty : a cross-national study. In* The many faces of crime and deviance. Israel studies in criminology. Vol. 6, Edited by S. Giora Shoham. White Plains, N.Y., Sherian House, 1983, p. 193-203.
Rahav, G. *Homicide and death penalty : cross-sectional time series analysis.* International Journal of Comparative and applied Criminal Justice. Wichita, KS, 7 : 61-71, 1983, no. 1-2.
Ramos Pedrueza, A. *Pena de muerte (Capital punishment).* Criminalia. México, D.F., 27 : 541-547, noviembre 1961.
Rankin, J.H. *Changing attitudes toward capital punishment.* Social Forces. Chapel Hill, N.C., 58 : 194-211, 1979, no. 1.
Rankin, J.H. *Investigating the interrelations among social control variables and conformity ; changing attitudes toward capital punishment ; schools and delinquency.* Ann. Arbor, MI, University Microfilms International, 1978.
Ratcliff, D. and Howell, R.J. *Gary Gilmore letters : a study of people who wrote to a condemned killer.* Salt Lake City, UT, Utah Division of Corrections research and Statistics, 1978, 37 p.
Rateau, M. *Les peines capitales et corporelles en France sous l'ancien régime (Capital and corporal punishments under the ancient regime in France).* Annales Internationales de Criminologie. Paris : 276-308, 1963.

Raux, M. *Les actes, l'attitude et la correspondance de Caserio en prison. Les transes, les angoisses et les anxiétés d'un condamné à mort (Actions, attitudes and correspondence by Caserio while in prison. Trances, fears and anxieties of a death sentenced individual).* Archives d'Anthropologie Criminelle et de Criminologie. Paris : 465-505, 1903.
Ray, J.J. *Attitude to the death penalty in South Africa – With some international comparison.* Journal of Social Psychology. Provincetown, MA, 116 : 287-288, 1982, no. 2.
Reaves, L. *Death row aid plea raises fuss in bar (Fla.).* Bar Leader. Chicago, IL, 10 : 23, January-February 1985.
Reckless, W.C. *The use of the death penalty.* Crime and Delinquency. Hackensack, N.J., 15 : 43-56, January 1969.
Redo, S. *The capital punishment question in the United Nations : recent developments.* Cahiers de Defense Sociale. Milan : 63-77, 1983.
Redo, S. *Zagadnienie kary śmierci (The problem of the death penalty). In* Problematyka przestepcośći na VI Kongresie ONZ. Edited by B. Holyst. Warszawa, 1983, p. 167-182.
Reeds, L.M.T. Furman v. Georgia and *Kentucky statutory law.* Kentucky Bar Journal. Frankfort, KY, 37 : 25, January 1973.
Reichert, W.O. *Capital punishment reconsidered.* Kentucky Law Journal. Lexington, KY, 47 : 397-419, Spring 1959.
Reik, T. *Freud's views on capital punishment. In* The compulsion to confess. By T. Reik. New York, N.Y., Books for Librairies Press Inc. 1959, p. 469-494.
Reiman, J.H. *Justice, civilisation and the death penalty : answering van den Haag,* Philosophy and Public Affairs. Princeton, N.J., 14 : 115-148, 1985, no. 2.
Reiman, J.H. and Headlee, S. *Marxism and criminal justice policy.* Crime and Delinquency. Hackensack, N.J., 27 : 24-47, 1981, no. 1.
Renda, E.A. *The bitter fruit of McGautha : Eddings v. Oklahoma and the need for weighing method articulation in capital sentencing.* American Criminal Law Review. Chicago, IL, 20 : 63-98, 1982, no. 1.
Rentoul, G. *Second thoughts on capital punishment.* Penal Reformer. London, 6, July 1939, no. 1.
Respuesta al cuestionario de Naciones Unidas sobre la pena de muerte en México (The answer to the UN questionnaire on capital punishment in Mexico). Para A. Quiroz Cuaron y otros. Derecho Penal Contemporaneo. Mexico, D.F., no. 15 : 55-81, julio-agosto 1966.
Restrepo, A.J. *La pena de muerte : texto íntegro de su intervencion en el Senado de la Republica de 1925 (The death penalty : the full text of his speech in the Senate in 1925).* Bogotá, Edición Publicitaria, s.d.
Resurrection the death penalty : the validity of Arizona's response to Furman v. Georgia. Arizona State Law Journal. Tempe, AZ : 257-296, 1974.
Revival of the eighth amendment : development of cruel-punishment doctrine by the Supreme Court. Stanford Law Review. Stanford, CA, 16 : 996-1015, July 1964.
Rhoads, M.D. *Resurrection of capital punishment : the 1976 death penalty cases.* Dickinson Law Review. Carlisle, PA, 81 : 543-573, 1977, no. 3.
Richards, R.C. *Death among the shifting standards : capital punishment*

after Furman. South Dakota Law Review. Vermillion, S.D., no. 26 : 243-258, Spring 1981.

Richert, J.P. *La peine de mort aux Etats-Unis (Rapport statistique sur les condamnations à mort) (Capital punishment in the U.S. Statistical report on death sentences).* Revue de Science Criminelle et de Droit Pénal Comparé. Paris : 1127-1129, octobre-decembre 1975.

Richey, L.K. *Death penalty statutes : a post-Gregg v. Georgia survey and discussion of eighth amendment safeguards.* Washburn Law Journal. Topeka, KS, 16 : 497-508, 1977, no. 2.

Rico, J.M. *La peine de mort, l'ordre et la sécurité publics : étude critique du projet de loi C-84 (Capital punishment and public safety : a critical study on the draft law C-84).* Canadian Journal of Criminology and Corrections. Ottawa, Ont., 19 : 230-242, April 1977.

Riedel, M. *Discrimination in the imposition of the death penalty : a comparison of the characteristics of offenders sentenced pre-Furman and post-Furman.* Telple Law Quarterly. Philadelphia, PA, 49 : 261-287, Winter 1976.

Riedel, M. and McCloskey, J.P. *The Governor's study commission on capital punishment.* Prison Journal. Philadelphia, PA, 53 : 19-35, Spring-Summer 1973.

Riedel, M. *The poor and capital punishment : some notes on social attitude.* Prison Journal. Philadelphia, PA, 45 : 24, Spring-Fall 1965.

Riedel, M. *Pre- and post-Furman comparisons and characteristics of offenders under death sentences. In* Capital punishment in the United States. Edited by H.A. Bedau and C.M. Pierce. New York, N.Y., AMS Press, 1976, p. 535-554.

Riga, P. *Capital punishment and the right to life : some reflections on the human right as absolute.* University of Puget Sound Law Review, 5 : 23-40, 1981.

Riley, K.W. *The death penalty in Georgia : an aggravating circumstance.* American University Law Review. Washington, D.C., 30 : 835-861, 1981, no. 3.

Riley, T.J. *The right of the state to inflict capital punishment.* Catholic Lawyer. Jamaica, N.Y. : 279-285, Fall 1960.

Ringold, S.M. *The dynamics of executive clemency.* American Bar Association Journal. Chicago, IL, 52 : 240-243, March 1966.

The Road to hell. Penal Reformer. London, 4, January 1938.

The Road up from barbarism. Social Service Review. Chicago, IL, 46 : 431-432, 1972, no. 3.

Roberts, J.V. *Public opinion and capital punishment : the effects of attitudes upon memory.* Canadian Journal of Criminology. Ottawa, Ont., 26 : 283-292, 1984, no. 3.

Robin, G.D. *The executioner : his place in English society.* British Journal of Sociology. London, 15 : 234-253, September 1964.

Rockefeller, W. *Executive clemency and the death penalty.* Catholic University Law Review, Washington, D.C., 21 : 94, Fall 1971.

Rodinson, M. *La pena di morte nella tradizione islamica (Capital punishment in Islamic tradition). In* La pena di morte nel mondo. By Amnesty International. Casale Monferrato, Marietti, 1983, p. 59-74.

Rodley, N. *La pena di morte nella legislazione internazionale sui diritti umani (Capital punishment in international laws on human rights). In* La pena di morte nel mondo. By Amnesty International. Casale Monferrato, Marietti, 1983, p. 153-174.
Roeleveld, L. *Capital punishment : a retentionist's views.* Speculum Juris. Fort Hare, 7 : 25-41, 1971-1972.
Rogers, J.W. *Let's ban capital punishment permanently. In* Critical issues in criminal justice. By R.G. Iacovetta and D.H. Chang. Durham, N.C., Carolina Academic Press, 1979.
Rogers, R.R. *The death penalty.* NLADA Briefcase. Chicago, IL, 34 : 1-9, 1976, no. 1.
Roll v. Larson : *The right to bail in capital cases after Furman v. Georgia.* Utah Law Review. Salt Lake City, UT : 421-432, Summer, 1974.
Romilly, H. *The punishment of death.* Ann Arbor, MI, Finch Press, 1886.
Roper, W.F. *Murderers in custody. In* The hanging question. Edited by L. Blom-Cooper. London, Duckworth and Co., 1969, p. 101-104.
Rose, G. *The struggle for penal reform.* London, Stevens and Sons Ltd., 1961, 328 p.
Rosenberg, D. and Levy, K. *Capital punishment : coming to grips with the dignity of man.* California Western Law Review. San Diego, CA, 14 : 275-297, 1978, no. 2.
Rosengarten, F. *25 lat pozbawienia wolności czy kara śmierci ? (25 years imprisonment or capital punishment ?)* Palestra. Warsaw, no. 2 : 80-83, 1984.
Ross, A. *Campaign against punishment.* Scandinavian Studies in Law. Stockholm, 14 : 111, 1970.
Rossa, K. *La peine de mort. L'histoire et la géographie de l'assassinat légal (Capital punishment. History and geography of legal murder).* Paris, Librairie Plon, 1966, 307 p.
Rossi, P. *La pena di morte : scetticismo e dogmatica (Capital punishment : scepticism and dogmatism).* Milano, Pan Editrice, 1978, 273 p.
Roucek, J.S. *Capital punishment : its legal and social aspects.* International Journal of Legal Research. Meerut Cantt., U.P., 6 : 49-66, 1971.
Rubin, S. *Imposition of death sentence for rape. In* The criminal in the arms of the law. Edited by L. Radzinowicz and M.E. Wolfgang. New York, N.Y., Basic Books, 1971.
Rubin, S. *The Supreme Court, cruel and unusual punishment, and the death penalty.* Crime and Delinquency. Hackensack, N.J., 15 : 121-131, January 1969.
Ruff, J.R. *Crime, justice and public order in old regime France.* Dover, N.H., Croom Helm, 1984, 211 p.
Rupp, J.C. *The last drop.* Forensic Science Gazette. Dallas, TX, 3 : 1-3, 1972, no. 1.
Rush, B. *Considerations on the injustice and impolicy of punishing murder by death. In* A plan for the punishment of crime by Benjamin Rush. Edited by N.K. Teeters. Philadelphia, PA, Prison Society, 1954.
Rush, D.P. *Constitutional law : Safeguarding eighth amendment rights with a comparative proportionality review in the imposition of the death penalty.* Howard Law Journal. Washington, D.C., 28 : 331-353, 1985, no. 1.

Ryan, S. *Capital punishment in Canada.* British Journal of Criminology. London, 9 : 80, 1969.
Ryding, P. *Nagra synpunkter pa debatten om doddstraffet (Points for a debate on capital punishment).* Nordisk Tidssfrift for Kriminalvidenskab. Kobenhavn, 49 : 305-308, 1961, no. 4.
Saito, S. *(Theory of abolishing capital punishment : pros and cons.)* Hòritsu Jiho. Japan, 42 : 16, May 1970. In Japanese.
Salkin, M. *The Furman decision and current death penalty legislation.* Georgia Journal of Corrections. Atlanta, GA, 3 : 10-25, August 1974.
Samuelson, G.W. *Why was capital punishment restored in Delaware ?* Journal of Criminal Law, Criminology and Police Science. Baltimore, MD, 60 : 148-151, June 1969.
Sanchez Oses, J. *La abolición de la pena de muerte (The abolition of capital punishment).* Anuario de Derecho Penal y Ciencias Penales. Madrid, 10 : 121-127, enero-abril 1957.
Sandoval Huertas, E. *Note sull'evoluzione storica della pena di morte in Colombia (Notes on the history of capital punishment in Colombia).* Dei Delitti e delle Pene. Napoli, 2 : 383-418, 1984, no. 2.
Santoro, A. *La pena di morte sul piano religioso e sul piano sociale (The death penalty from a religious and social point of view).* Scuola Positiva. Milano : 28-30, 1961.
Sarat, A. and Vidmar, N. *Public opinion, the death penalty, and the eighth amendment : testing the Marshall hypothesis.* Wisconsin Law Review. Madison, WI : 171-206, 1976. Also in Capital punishment in the United States. Edited by H.A. Bedau and C.M. Pierce. New York, N.Y., AMS Press, 1976, p. 190-224.
Savey-Casard, P. *L'eglise catholique et la peine de mort (The catholic church and capital punishment).* Revue de Science Criminelle et de Droit Pénal Comparé. Paris : 773-785, octobre-decembre 1961.
Savey-Casard, P. *La peine de mort. Esquisse historique et juridique (Capital punishment : historical and legal sketch).* Genève, Librairie Droz, 1968, 179 p.
Savey-Casard, P. *Peut-on remplacer la peine de mort ? (Can capital punishment be replaced ?)* Revue Penitentiaire et de Droit Pénal. Paris : 545-572, octobre-decembre 1977.
Savitz, L.D. *Capital crimes as defined in American statutory law.* Journal of Criminal Law, Criminology and Police Science. Baltimore, MD, 46 : 355-363, September-October 1955.
Savitz, L.D. *The deterrent effect of capital punishment in Philadelphia. In* The death penalty in America ; an Anthology. Edited by H.A. Bedau. Garden City, N.Y., Anchor Books, 1964, p. 315-322.
Savitz, L.D. *A study in capital punishment.* Journal of Criminal Law, Criminology and Police Science. Baltimore, MD, 49 : 338-341, November-December 1958.
Scaduto, A. *Scapegoat : the lonesome death of Bruno Richard Hauptman.* New York, N.Y., Putnam, 1976, 512 p.
Schedler, G. *Capital punishment and its deterrent effect.* Social Theory and Practice. Tallahassee, FL, 4 : 47-56, 1976, no. 1.
Schierbeck, O. *Dodsdomt (Capital punishment).* Kobenhavn, 1974, 192 p.

Schloss, B. and Giesbrecht, N.A. *Murder in Canada : a report on capital and non-capital murder statistics, 1961-1970.* Toronto, Ont., Centre of Criminology, University of Toronto, 1972, 96 p.
Schoenfeld, C.G. *The desire to abolish capital punishment : a psychoanalytically-oriented analysis.* Journal of Psychiatry and Law. New York, N.Y., 11 : 151-181, 1983, no. 2.
Schofield, G.R. *Due process in the United States Supreme Court and the death of the Texas capital murder statute.* American Journal of Criminal Law. Austin, TX, 8 : 1-42, 1980, no. 1.
Schuessler, K. *The deterrent influence of the death penalty.* Annals of the American Academy of Political and Social Science. Philadelphia, PA, 284 : 54-62, November 1952.
Schultz, M.L. *Eighth amendment : references to appellate review of capital sentencing determinations :* Caldwell v. Mississippi 105S. Ct. 2633 (1985). Journal of Criminal Law and Criminology. Chicago, IL, 76 : 1051-1064, Winter 1985.
Schurmann Pacheco, R. *The death penalty in Uruguay.* Crime Prevention and Criminal Justice Newsletter. Vienna, no. 12/13 : 32-38, November 1986.
Schuster, M. *L'abolition de la peine de mort en Angleterre et la défense sociale (The abolition of capital punishment in England and social defence).* Bulletin de la Société Internationale de Défense Sociale. Milan, no. 2 : 17-20, 1955.
Schwab, H.J. *Legislating a death penalty.* Lexington, KY, Council of State Governments, 1977, 22 p.
Schwartz, D. *Diagnosing the death sentence for felony murder on a non-triggerman.* Stanford Law Review. Stanford, CA, 37 : 857-888.
Schwartz, L.B. *Crime and the American penal system.* Annals of the American Academy of Political and Social Science. Philadelphia, PA, 339 : 1-170, January 1962.
Schwarzschild, H. *In opposition to death penalty legislation. In* The death penalty in America. Edited by H.A. Bedau, 3rd ed. Oxford. Oxford University Press, 1982, p. 364-369.
Schwarzschild, S.S. *Kantianism on the death penalty (and related social problems).* Archiv fuer Rechts – und Sozialphilosophie. Wiesbaden, 71 : 343-372, 1985, no. 3.
Schwed, R.E. *Abolition and capital punishment : the United States' judicial, political and moral barometer.* New York, N.Y., AMS Press, 1983, 238 p.
Scott, G.R. *The history of capital punishment.* London, Torchstream Publishing Ltd., 1950, 312 p.
Seagle, W. *Acquitted of murder.* Chicago, IL, Henry Regnery, 1958.
Sebba, L. *The pardoning power : a world survery.* Journal of Criminal Law and Criminology. Chicago, IL, 68 : 83, 1977.
Seguin, D. and Horowitz, J. *The effects of « death qualification » on juror and jury decisioning : an analysis from three perspectives.* Law and Human Behavior. New York, N.Y., 8 : 95-115, 1984.
Sellin, T. *Capital punishment.* Federal Probation. Washington, D.C., 25 : 3-11, September 1961.

Sellin, T. *Capital punishment.* Crime Prevention and Criminal Justice Newsletter. Vienna, no. 12/13 : 5-9, November 1986.
Sellin, T. ed. *Capital punishment.* New York, N.Y., Harper and Row, 1967, 290 p.
Sellin, T. *Capital punishment. In* Readings in criminology and penology. By D. Dressler. New York, N.Y., Columbia University Press, 1964, p. 489-504.
Sellin, T. *Death and imprisonment as deterrents to murder. In* The death penalty in American ; an anthology. Edited by H.A. Bedau. Garden City, N.Y., Anchor Books, 1964, p. 274-284.
Sellin, T. *The death penalty : a report for the model penal code project of the America Law Institute.* Philadelphia, PA, The American Law Institute, 1959, 84 p.
Sellin, T. *The death penalty : retribution or deterrence. In* Report for 1976 and Resource Material Series no. 13. Tokyo, UNAFEI, 1977, p. 41-52.
Sellin, T. *Les débats concernant l'abolition de la peine capitale : une retrospective (Debates on the abolition of capital punishment : a retrospective view).* Déviance et Société. Genève, 5 : 97-112, 1981.
Sellin, T. *Does the death penalty protect municipal police ? In* The death penalty in America ; an anthology. Edited by H.A. Bedau. Garden City, N.Y., Anchor Books, 1964, p. 284-301.
Sellin, T. *Effect of repeal and reintroduction of the death penalty on homicide rates. In* The death penalty in America ; an anthology. Edited by H.A. Bedau. Garden City, N.Y., Anchor Books, 1964, p. 339-343.
Sellin, T. *Experiments with abolition. In* Capital punishment. Edited by T. Sellin. New York, N.Y., Harper and Row, 1967, p. 122-124.
Sellin, T. *Homicides in retentionist and abolitionist states. In* Capital punishment. Edited by T. Sellin. New York, N.Y., Harper and Row, 1967, p. 135-138.
Sellin, T. *Intimidation générale et peine de mort (General deterrence and capital punishment).* Revue de droit Pénal et de Criminologie. Bruxelles, 59 : 315-325, 1979.
Sellin, T. ed. *Murder and the death penalty.* Annals of the American Academy of Political and Social Science. Philadelphia, PA, 284 : 1-166. 231-238, November 1952.
Sellin, T. *A note on capital executions in the United States.* British Journal of Criminology. London, 1 : 6-14, July 1950.
Sellin, T. *La peine de mort aux Etats Unies : état actuel de la question (Capital punishment in the United States : present status of the question).* Revue de Droit Pénal et de Criminologie. Bruxelles, 49 : 706-711, avril 1969.
Sellin, T. *La peine de mort et le meurtre (Capital punishment and murder).* Revue de Science Criminelle et de Droit Pénal Comparé. Paris : 739-767, 1957.
Sellin, T. *The penalty of death.* Beverly Hills, Ca, Sage Publications, 1980, 190 p.
Sellin, T. *Two myths in the history of capital punishment.* Journal of Criminal Law, Criminology and Police Science. Baltimore, MD, 50 : 114-117, July-August 1959.
Sentence of death in Trinidad and Tobago – Fundamental rights and free-

doms under the Constitution – Prerogative of mercy – Whether right to have advisory committee's report disclosed. Criminal Law Review. London : 50-51, January 1976.
Separovic, Z. *Psihopatske (sociopatske) licnosti i smrtna kazna (Psychopaths (sociopaths) and the death penalty).* Psuhologija licnosti (Zbornik). Zagreb : 163-179, 1972.
Sequin, D.G. and Horowitz I.A. *The effects of " death qualification " on juror and jury decisioning : an analysis from three perspectives.* Law and Psychology Review. University, AL, 8 : 49-81, Spring 1984.
Serrano Gomez, A. *Consideraciones criminologicas sobre los efectos de la abolición de la pena de muerte en Espana (Criminological considerations on the abolition of the death penalty in Spain).* Anuario de Derecho Penal y Ciencias Penales. Madrid, 35 : 609-625, 1982, no. 2.
Serrano Gomez, A. *La pena de muerte en el Real Decreto-Ley 45/1978, de 21 de Diciembre (Capital punishment in the Royal Decree 45/1978 of 21 December).* Revista de Estudios Penitenciarios. Madrid, no. 228-231 : 275-280, 1980.
Sesnowitz, M. and McKee, D. *On the deterrent effect of capital punishment.* Journal of Behavioral Economics. Macomb, IL, 6 : 217-224, 1977.
Seth, I. *Overheten och svardet : doddstraffdebatten i Sverige 1809-1974 (Questions and answers : debates on capital punishment in Sweden 1809-1974).* Stockholm, Nordiska Bokhandeln, 1984, 340 p.
The Shadow of the gallows. By S. Templewood and others. London, Victor Gollancz Ltd., 1951.
Shaffer, H.B. *Death penalty.* Editorial Research Reports. Washington, D.C. : 573-588, 1953.
Shalloo, J.P. ed. *Crime in the United States.* Annals of the American Academy of Political and Social Science. Philadelphia, PA, 217 : 1-163, September 1941.
Sharp, M.P. *Was justice done ? The Rosenberg-Sobell case.* New York, N.Y., Monthly Review Press, 1956, 216 p.
Shaw, A.M.N. *The penalty for murder and judges' recommendations.* Howard Journal of Penology and Crime Prevention. London, 15 : 31-49, 1976.
Shaw, G.B. *The crime of imprisonment.* New York, N.Y., Philosophical Library, 1946, 125 p.
Sheehan, T.M. *Administrative review and capital punishment : the Canadian concept.* American Journal of Correction. St. Paul, MN, 27 : 24-25, January-February 1965.
Shin, K. *Death penalty and crime : empirical studies.* Fairfax, VA, George Mason University, 1978, 279 p.
Showalter, C.R. and Bonnier, R. *Psychiatrists and capital sentencing : risks and responsabilities in a unique legal setting.* Bulletin of the American Academy of Psychiatry and the Law. Pittsburgh, PA, 12 : 159-167, 1984.
Silas, F. *On death row : should children be executed ?* American Bar Association Journal. Chicago, IL, 72 : 26, March 1986.
Sindwani, K.L. *Crime and penal institutions in New Zealand.* Criminology. Beverly Hills, CA, 9 : 330, August-November 1971.
Singh, A. *Attitudes of Canadians toward crime and punishment.* Cana-

dian Journal of Criminology. Ottawa, Ont., 21 : 463-466, October 1979.
Singh, A. and Jayewardene, C.H.S. *Philosophical consistency in public attitudes on crime and justice.* Australian and New Zealand Journal of Criminology. Melbourne, Victoria, 11 : 182-184, 1978, no. 3.
Skinner, M.M. *The question of capital punishment.* Lincoln, NE, 1976, 201 p.
Slovenko, R. *And the penalty is (sometimes) death.* Antioch Review. Yellow Springs, OH : 351-364, 1964.
Slowik, A. *Stosowanie kary smierci w swoetle prac ONZ (The application of the death penalty in the light of UN activities).* Zeszyty Naukowe Akademii Spraw Wewnetrznych no. 43, 1986.
Smith, C.E. and Felix, R.R. *Beyond deterrence : a study of defenses on death row.* Federal Probation. Washington, D.C., 50 : 55-59, September 1986.
Smith, E. *Brief against death.* New York, N.Y., Avon Books, 1969, 352 p.
Smith, G.W. *The value of life – Arguments against the death penalty : a reply to Professor Lehtinen.* Crime and Delinquency. Hackensack, N.J., 23 : 253-259, July 1977.
Smith, M. *Concordance in change of attitude with reference to war and capital punishment.* Journal of Social Psychology. Provincetown, MA, 12 : 379-386, 1940.
Smith, M.H. *The shame of capital punishment.* Penal Reformer. London, 1. January 1935.
Smith, N.B. *The death penalty as an unconstitutional deprivation of life and the right to privacy.* Boston College Law Review. Boston, MA, 25 : 743-761, 1984.
Smith, T.W. *A trend analysis of attitudes toward capital punishment, 1936-1974. In* Studies of social change since 1948. Edited by J.A. Davis, vol. 2 Chicago, IL, Chicago University Press, 1975, p. 257-318.
Snyder, O.C. *Capital punishment : the moral issue.* West Virginia Law Review. Morgantown, VA, 63 : 99, 1961.
Society of Friends. Conference on Crime and the Treatment of Offenders. Continuation Committee. What do the churches say on capital punishment ? 7th ed. Philadelphia, PA, Friends World Committee, 1960-61, 64 p.
Society today : moral battlegrounds. New Society. London, 55 : I-IV, 1981, no. 957.
Solnar, V. *Tresty a ochrawna opatreni (Punishments and protective measures). In* System ceskoslovenskeho trestniho prava. By V. Solnar. Praha, 1979, p. 117-120.
Solomon, G.F. *Capital punishment as suicide and as murder.* American Journal of Orthopsychiatry. Albany, N.Y., 45 : 701-711, 1975, no. 4. Also in Capital punishment in the United States. Edited by H.A. Bedau and C.M. Pierce. New York, N.Y., AMS Press, 1976, p. 432-444.
Some reflections on punishment. Penal Reformer. London, 5, October 1938.
Spangler, J.A. *California's death penalty dilemma.* Crime and Delinquency. Hackensack, N.J., 15 : 142-148, 1969, no. 1.
Speaker, F. *Capital punishment : ineffective, unjust, unconstitutional.* Prison Journal. Philadelphia, PA, 53 : 36-48, Spring-Summer 1973.

Spear, C. *Punishment of death.* London, John Green, 1844, 115 p.
The Special case of capital punishment. In The growth of crime. By L. Radzinowicz and J. King. New York, N.Y., Basic Books Inc., 1977, p. 142-148.
Specter, A. *Minority report in support of the reinstitution of capital punishment.* Philadelphia, PA, Governor's Study Commission on Capital Punishment, 1973.
Spielmann, A. *La peine de mort au Grand-Duché de Luxembourg (The death penalty in Luxembourg).* Revue de Science Criminelle et de Droit Pénale Comparé. Paris : 661-692, juillet-septembre 1976.
Spierenburg, P. *The spectacle of suffering : executions and the evolution of repression from a preindustrial metropolis to the European experience.* New York, N.Y., Cambridge University Press, 1984, 274 p.
Sprott, W.J.H. *Conflicts of values. In* The Hanging question. Edited by L. Blom-Cooper. London, Duckworth and Co., 1969, p. 21-28.
Sramota, W. *Reactions of criminals and political prisoners to impending death sentences.* Journal of Offender Therapy. New York, N.Y., 6 : 40-46, September 1962.
Sri Lanka. *Commission of Inquiry on Capital Punishment.* Report. Colombo, Government Press, 1959, 118 p.
Srivastava, O.P. *Problems and perspectives in death sentence.* Social Defence. New Delhi, 14 : 15-20, no. 53.
Ssekandi, F.M. *Uganda and Kondos : the capital punishment revisited.* Eastern African Law Review. Dar es Salaam, 3 : 83-95, April 1970.
Stacy, R.L. *Is the death penalty dead ?* Baylor Law Review. Waco, TX, 26 : 114-122, 1974, no. 1.
Statistical evidence on the deterrent effect of capital punishment. Yale Law Journal. New Haven, CT, 85 : 164-227, 1975, no. 2.
Status of the death penalty : constitutional restrictions on the imposition of capital punishment. Wake Forest Intramural Law Review (now Wake Forest Law Review). Winston-Salem, N.C., 5 : 183-196, 1969.
Stein, G.M. *Distinguishing among murders when assessing the proportionality of death penalty.* Columbia Law Review. Irvington, N.Y., 85 : 1786-1807, 1985, no. 8.
Stevens, L.A. *Death penalty : the case of life vs. death in the United States.* New York, N.Y., Coward, McCann and Geoghegan Inc., 1978.
Steyn, J.H. *The punishment scene in South Africa – Developments over the past decade and the prospects for reform. In* Crime, Criminology and Public Policy. Edited by R. Hood. London, Heinemann Educational Books Ltd., 1974, p. 527-570.
Strada, V. *La pena di morte e le rivoluzioni russe (The death penalty and the Russian revolutions). In* La pena di morte nel mondo By Amnesty International. Casale Monteferrato, Marietti, 1983, p. 135-152.
Strafer, G.R. *Volunteering for execution : competency, voluntariness and propriety of third party intervention.* The Journal of Criminal Law and Criminology. Chicago, IL, 74 : 860-912, 1983, no. 3.
Strategies of abolition. Yale Law Journal. New Haven, CT, 84 : 1769-1778, July 1975.
Strauss, F. *Where did justice go ?* Boston, MA, Gambit Inc., 1970, 228 p.

Streib, V.L. *Capital punishment for children in Ohio.* Akron Law Review. Akron, OH, 18 : 51-102, 1984.

Streib, V.L. *Death penalty for children : the American experience with capital punishment for crimes committed while under age eighteen.* Oklahoma Law Review. Aklahoma City, OK, 36 : 613-641, 1983, no. 3.

Streib, V.L. *Executions under the post-Furman capital punishment statutes : the halting progression from « Let's do it » to « Hey, there ain't no point in pulling so tight ».* Rutgers Law Journal. Camden, N.J., 443-487, 1984, no. 15.

Stricker, G. and Jurow, G.L. *The relationship between attitudes toward capital punishment and assignment of the death penalty.* Journal of Psychiatry and Law. New York, N.Y., 2 : 415-422, 1974, no. 4.

Strom, F. *On the sacral origin of the Germanic death penalties.* Lund, Makan Ohlssons, 1942.

Subramanyam, K.G. *Can the state kill its citizen ?* Madras, Law Journal Office, 1969, 70 p.

Suchy, O.L. *Namety na prohlubeni diferenciace a individualizace trestu a ochrannych opatreni (Reasons for the increasing differentiation and individualization of punishments and protective measures).* Serie Kriminologicky Institut CSSR, no. 4 : 80, 1981.

La Suède et la peine de mort (Sweden and the death penalty). Revue de Science Criminelle et de Droit Pénal Comparé. Paris : 201, janvier-mars 1973.

Sueiro Rodriguez, D. *El arte de matar (The art of killing).* 2nd ed. Madrid-Barcelona. Edigens, 1979, 768 p.

Sueiro Rodriguez, D. *La pena de muerte : ceremonial, historia, procedimientos (The death penalty : ceremonies, history, procedures).* Madrid, Alianza Editorial, 1974.

Sufrin, R. *" Everything is in order, Warden' : a discussion of death in the gas chamber.* Suicide. New York, N.Y., 6 : 44-57, 1976, no. 1.

Sumiya, A.A. *(Materials concerning capital punishment).* Osaka Law Review. Osaka, 66 : 65-112, 1968. In Japanese.

The Supreme Court and the death penalty : the effects of judicial choice on legislative options. Boston University Law review. Boston, MA, 54 : 158-185, January 1974.

Survival of the death penalty. Baylor Law Review. Waco, TX, 23 : 499, Summer 1971.

Susini, J. *La police et la peine de mort (The police and capital punishment).* Revue de Science Criminelle et de Droit Pénal Comparé. Paris : 512-516, 1960.

Sutherland, E.H. *Murder and the death penalty.* Journal of Criminal Law, Criminology and Police Science. Baltimore, MD, 15 : 520-529, February 1925.

Suyver, J.J.H. *Doodstraf in het militair strafrecht en de wetgeving inzake oorlogsmisdrijven en misdrijven tegen de menselijkheid (Nederland) (Capital punishment in military criminal law...)* Nederlands Juristenblad. Zwolle, 56 : 1209, 1981, no. 45/46.

Switka, J. *Refleksje o karze śmierci w swietle teorii penalnych (Reflections*

on the death penalty in the light of penal theories). Nowe Prawo. Warsaw, no. 3 : 58-75, 1986.
Switzerland and the death penalty. Penal Reform News. Pretoria : 8-10, July 1952.
Symposium on current death penalty issues. Journal of Criminal Law and Criminology. Chicago, IL, 74, 1983, no. 3.
Symposium on the death penalty. By P.C. Davis and others. Criminals Law Bulletin. Boston, MA, 14 : 5-80, 1978, no. 1.
Szasz, T.W. *Law, liberty, and psychiatry.* New York, N.Y., Collier, 1968.
Zsumski, B., L. *Hall and S. Bursell, eds. The death penalty : opposing viewpoints.* St. Paul, MN, Greenhaven Press, 1986.
Talbot, C.K. *Capitalism and capital punishment : an historical note on the Westinghouse/Edison Debate of 1890.* Crime et/and Justice. Ottawa, Ont., 6 : 129-133, 1978, no. 2.
Tao, L.S. Beyond Furman v. Georgia : *The need for a morally based decision on capital punishment.* Notre Dame Lawyer. Notre Dame, IN, 51 : 722-736, April 1976.
Tarde, G. *La philosophie pénale (Penal phylosophy).* Paris-Lyon, Stock-Masson, 1890.
Tarlat, J. *La peine de mort en question (Questioning the death penalty).* Paris, Editions Pygmalion, 1977, 254 p.
Teeters, N.K. and Zibulka, C.J. *Executions under state authority : an inventory. In* Executions in America. By W.J. Bowers. Lexington, MA, D.C. Heath and Co., 1974, p. 200-401.
Teeters, N.K. and Hedblom, J.H. *Hang by the neck. The legal use of scaffold and noose, gibbet, stake and firing squad from colonial times to the present.* Springfield, IL, Charles C. Thomas, 1967, 483 p.
Teeters, N.K. *Public executions in Philadelphia.* Prison Journal. Philadelphia, PA, 53 : 58-71, Spring-Summer 1973.
Teeters, N.K. *Scaffold and chair : a compilation of their use in Pennsylvania, 1682-1962.* Philadelphia, PA, Prison Society, 1963.
Teevan Jr., J.J. *Deterrent effects of punishment : subjective measures continued.* Canadian Journal of Criminology and Corrections. Ottawa, Ont., 18 : 152-160, April 1976.
Teevan JR., J.J. *Deterrent effects of punishment : the Canadian case.* Canadian Journal of Criminology and Corrections. Ottawa, Ont., 14 : 68-82, January 1972.
Templewood, V. *The shadow of the gallows.* London. Victor Gollancz, 1951.
Tena Fatas, G. *Consideraciones sobre la pena capital (Considerations on capital punishment).* Policia Espanola. Madrid, 9 : 17-20, 1970.
Terry, S. *The death penalty : an issue that won't die.* Law Enforcement Journal. Bethel Island, CA : 6-7, May 1979.
Thibault, L. *La peine de mort en France et à l'étranger (The death penalty in France and abroad).* Paris, Gallimard, 1977, 248 p.
Thomas, C.W. *Eighth amendment challenges to the death penalty : the relevance of informed public opinion.* Vanderbilt Law Review. Nashville, TN, 30 : 1005-1030, 1977, no. 5.
Thomas, C.W. and Howard, R. *Public attitudes towards capital punish-*

ment : a comparative analysis. Journal of Behavioral Economics. Macomb, IL, 6 : 189-216, 1977.
Thomas, C.W. and Foster, S.C. *A sociological perspective on public support for capital punishment.* American Journal of Orthopsychiatry. Albany, N.Y., 45 : 641-657, 1975, no. 4. Also in Capital punishment in the United States. Edited by H.A. Bedau and C.M. Pierce. New York, N.Y., AMS Press, 1976, p. 152-171.
Thomas, D.A. *Developments in sentencing.* Criminal Law Review. London : 685-692, December 1974.
Thomas, P.A. *Attitudes of wardens toward the death penalty. In* The death penalty in America ; an anthology. Edited by H.A. Bedau. Garden City, N.Y., Anchor Books, 1964, p. 242-252.
Thomas, P.A. *Murder and the death penalty.* American Journal of Correction. St. Paul, MN, 19 : 16-17, 30-32, July-August 1957.
Thomas, T. *This life we take.* 4th rev. San Francisco, CA, Friends Committee on Legislation, 1970.
Thompson, M. *The ethics of capital punishment.* Codicillus. Pretoria, 10 : 4-5, 1969, no. 1.
Thompson, R. *L'abolition de la peine de mort en Nouvelle-Zélande (The abolition of the death penalty in New Zealand).* Revue de Science Criminelle et de Droit Pénal Comparé. Paris, 17 : 83-88, janvier-mars 1962.
Thompson, R. *Le rétablissement de la peine capitale en Nouvelle-Zélande (The restablishment of the death penalty in New Zealand).* Revue de Science Criminelle et de Droit Pénal Comparé. Paris : 821-827, 1957.
Thompson, W.C. *Death penalty attitudes and conviction proneness : the translation of attitudes into verdicts.* Law and Human Behavior. New York, N.Y., 8 : 95-113, 1984, no. 1/2.
Thonisson, J.J. *Etudes sur l'histoire du droit criminel dans les pays anciens (Studies on the history of criminal law in ancient countries).* Brussels-Paris, Bruylant-Durand, 1869.
Thornton, T.P. *Terrorism and the death penalty. In* The death penalty in America. Edited by H.A. Bedau, 3rd ed. Oxford. Oxford University Press, 1982, p. 181-185.
Tidmarsh, M., Halloran, J.D. and Connolly, K.J. *Capital punishment : a case for abolition.* London - New York, Sheed and Ward Ltd., 1963.
Tifft, L. *Capital punishment research, policy and ethics ; defining murder and placing murderers.* Crime and Social Justice. Berkeley, CA, no. 17 : 61-68, 1982.
Tifft, L. *Reflections on capital punishment and the " campaign against crime " in the People's Republic of China.* Justice Quarterly. Lincoln, NE, 2 : 127-137, 1985, no. 1.
Timaeus, D. *Fourteenth amendment – Due process – Texas Penal Code, Section 12.31 (b). Inconstitutionality permits the exclusion for cause of jurors who have general objections to, or religious or moral scruples against the death penalty.* Adams v. Texas 448 U.S. 38 (1980). American Journal of Criminal Law. Austin, TX, 9 : 251-269, 1981, no. 2.
Tittle, C. *Crime rates and legal sanctions.* Social problems. South Bend, IN, 16 : 409-422, Spring 1969.
Tomic, M. *Kapitalna krivicna dela, sankcionisana smrtnom kaznom u kri-*

vicnim zakonima jugoslovenskin zemalja od 1804-1941 (Capital crimes in the criminal codes of Yugoslav countries, 1804-1941). Godisnjak Pravnog Fakulteta. Sarajevo, Bawalvka, no. 283-285, 1983.

Tomic, M. *Pogled na rezultate nekoloko anketa o smrtnoj kazni (Reflections on the public opinion survey regarding capital punishment).* Pravna Misao, no. 12 : 98-104, 1981.

Topping, C.W. *The death penalty in Canada.* Annals of the American Academy of Political and Social Science. Philadelphia, PA : 147-158, November 1952.

Torío A. *Beccaria y la inquisición espanola (Beccaria and the Spanish inquisition).* Anuario de Derecho Penal y Ciencias penales. Madrid, 24 : 391-415, mayo-agosto 1971.

Toulat, J. *La peine de mort en question (Questioning the death penalty).* Paris, 1977, 253 p.

Toulemon, A. *Un châtiment des crimes politiques (A punishment for political crimes).* Recueil de Droit Pénal. Paris : 27 : 281-284, 1969, no. 171.

Trepanier, J. *The administration of justice in Quebec : three new surveys.* British Journal of Criminology. London, 11 : 290-293, July 1971.

Triche, C.W. *The capital punishment dilemma, 1950-1977 : a subject bibliography.* Troy, N.Y., Whitston Publishing Co Inc., 1979, 278 p.

Tucker, C.B. *Capital punishment : a study of law and social structure.* Ann Arbor, MI, 1974, 211 p.

Tullock, G. *Does punishment deter crime.* Public Interest. New York, N.Y., no. 36 : 103-111, Summer 1974.

Turnaturi, G. *Orientamenti e tendenze sulla pena di morte (Trends regarding capital punishment).* Archivio Penale. Roma, 24 : 469-487, 1968.

Turnbull, C. *Death by decree : an anthropological approach to capital punishment.* Natural History. New York, N.Y., 87 : 51-67, 1978, no. 5.

Tuttle, E. *The crusade against capital punishment in Great Britain.* London, Stevens and Sons Ltd., 1961, 177 p.

Tyler, T.R. and Weber, R. *Support for the death penalty ; instrumental response to crime, or symbolic attitude ?* Law and Society Review. Denver, CO, 17 : 21-46, 1982, no. 1.

Tysoe, M. *And if we hanged the wrong man ?* New Society. London, 65 : 11-13, 1983, no. 1077.

Ulate, R. *The death penalty : some observations on Latin America.* Crime Prevention and Criminal Justice Newsletter. Vienna, no. 12-13 : 27-31, November 1986.

United Kingdom. Royal Commission on Capital Punishment. Minutes of evidence. London, H.M.S.O., 1949-1951, 678 p.

United Kingdom. Report. London, H.M.S.O., 1953, 505 p.

United Kingdom. Report, together with the minutes of evidence and appendix. London, H.M.S.O., 1966, 671 p.

United Kingdom :decisive vote against restoring death penalty. Amnesty International Newsletter. London, 13 : 7, 1983, no. 8.

United Nations. Commission for Social Development. Capital punishment. In Report of the Committee on Crime Prevention and Control on its third session. 7 November 1974, p. 42 (E/CN.5/516).

United Nations. Commission for Social Development. Capital punishment.

In Report of the Committee on Crime Prevention and Control on its fourth session. 15 October 1976, p. 17 (E/CN.5/536).
United Nations. Commission for Social Development. Capital punishment. In Report of the Committee on Crime Prevention and Control on its fifth session. 30 November 1978, p. 27 (E/CN.5/558).
United Nations. Commission for Social Development. Capital punishment. Report of the Committee on Crime Prevention and Control on its seventh session, held in Vienna, from 15 to 24 March 1982, 19 May 1982, 47, 5 p. (E/CN.5/1982/2).
United Nations. Commission on Human Rights. Capital punishment in the Republic of South Africa. In Report of the Ad Hoc Working Group of Experts on the Investigation requested in Resolution 21 (XXV) of the Commission on Human Rights. 27 January 1970, p. 27-29. (E/CN.4/1020).
United Nations. Commission for Social Development. Elaboration of a second optional protocol to the International Covenant on Civil and Political Rights, aiming at the abolition of the death penalty (E/CN.4/RES/1984/19). In Economic and Social Council Official Records. 1984, Suppl. no. 4, p. 54-55.
United Nations. Commission on Human Rights. International standards relating to capital punishment. In Report of the Ad Hoc Working Group of Experts on the Investigation requested in Resolution 21 (XXV) of the Commission o Human Rights. 27 January 1970, p. 13-14 (E/CN.4/1020).
United Nations. Commission on Human Rights. Committee on Crime Prevention and Control. Capital punishment. Note by the Secretary-General. 23 July 1974, 5 p. (E/AC.57/18).
United Nations. Commission on Human Rights. Capital punishment. In Progress report of the United Nations activities in crime prevention and control – Report of the Secretary-General. 27 April 1973, p. 1-2 (E/AC.57/12).
United Nations. Commission on Human Rights. Committee on Crime Prevention and Control : report on the eighth session, Vienna 21-30 March 1984, 83 p. (E/AC.57/1984/18).
United Nations. Department of Economic and Social Affairs Capital punishment. 1962, 76 p. 6Sales n° 67, IV, 15).
United Nations. Capital punishment : Part I. Report, 1960 ; *Part II.* Developments, 1961-1965, 1968, 134 p. (Sales no. 67, IV, 15).
United Nations. Commission on Human Rights. Capital punishment. In Report of the United Nations Consultative Group on the Prevention of Crime and the Treatment of Offenders. Geneva, 6-16 August 1968, 1968, p. 29-35 (Sales no. 69, IV, 3).
United Nations. Department of International Economic and Social Affairs. Capital punishment. In Sixth United Nations Congress on the Prevention of Crime and the Treatment of Offenders, Caracas, 25 August – 5 September 1980, p. 50 (Sales no. 81, IV, 4).
United Nations. Commission on Human Rights. Safeguards guaranteeing the rights of those facing death penalty. In Seventh United Nations Congress on the Prevention of Crime and the Treatment of Offenders, Milan, 26 August – 6 September 1985. Report prepared by the Secretariat.

February 1986, p. 83-84 (Sales no. 86, IV, 1).
United Nations. Economic and Social Council. Capital punishment. (E/RES/934), 9 April 1963. *In* Economic and Social Council Official Records, 35th Session, 1963, suppl. 1, p. 5-6.
United Nations. Economic and Social Council. Capital punishment. (E/RES/1243), 6 June 1967. In Economic and Social Council Official Records, 42nd Session, 1967, suppl. 1, p. 20-21.
United Nations. Economic and Social Council. Capital punishment. (E/RES/1337), 31 May 1968. In Official Records, 44th Session, 1968, suppl. 1, p. 19-20.
United Nations. Economic and Social Council. Capital punishment. (E/RES/1574), 20 May 1971. In Economic and Social Council Official Records, 50th Session, 1971, suppl. 1, p.7.
United Nations. Economic and Social Council. Capital punishment. (E/RES/1656), 1 June 1972. In Economic and Social Council Official Records, 52nd Session, 1972, suppl. 1, p.1.
United Nations. Economic and Social Council. Capital punishment. (E/RES/1745), 16 May 1973. In Economic and Social Council Official Records, 54th Session, 1973, suppl. 1, p.4.
United Nations. Economic and Social Council. Capital punishment. (E/RES/1930), 6 May 1975. In Economic and Social Council Official Records, 58th Session, 1975, suppl. 1, p. 35-36.
United Nations. Economic and Social Council. Capital punishment. (E/RES/1979/22). Economic and Social Council Official Records, 1979, suppl. 1, p. 17.
United Nations. Economic and Social Council. Capital punishment. (E/RES/1985/33). In Resolutions and decisions adopted by the Economic and Social Council at its 1st regular session of 1985, 12 June 1985, p. 59-60 (E/1985/INF/4).
United Nations. Economic and Social Council. Capital punishment. Note by the Secretary-General, 23 February 1971, 12 p. (E/4947).
United Nations. Economic and Social Council. Capital punishment. Note by the Secretary-General – Addendum, 20 September 1971. (E/4947/Add. 1).
United Nations. Economic and Social Council. Capital punishment. Note by the Secretary-General, 15 March 1972, 2 p. (E/5108).
United Nations. Economic and Social Council. Capital punishment. Report of the Secretary-General, 23 February 1973, 28 p. (E/5242).
United Nations. Economic and Social Council. Capital punishment. Report of the Secretary-General – Addendum, 19 March 1973, 1 p. (E/5242. Add. 1).
United Nations. Economic and Social Council. Capital punishment. Report of the Secretary-General, 12 February 1975, 15 p. (E/5616).
United Nations. Economic and Social Council. Capital punishment. Report of the Secretary-General – Addendum, 18 April 1975, 2 p. (E/5616/Add. 1).
United Nations. Economic and Social Council. Capital punishment. Report of the Secretary-General, 29 April 1971, 3 p. (E/4993).

United Nations. Economic and Social Council. Capital punishment. Report of the Social Committee, 24 April 1973, 6 p. (E/5298).
United Nations. Economic and Social Council. Capital punishment. Note by the Secretary-General, 1 May 1978, 7 p. (E/AC.57/33).
United Nations. Economic and Social Council. Elaboration of a 2nd optional protocol to the International Covenant on Civil and Political Rights, aiming at the abolition of the death penalty. (E/RES/1985/41). In Resolutions and decisions adopted by the Economic and Social Council at its 1st regular session of 1985, 7-31 May 1985. (E/RES/INF/4), 12 June 1985, p. 70.
United Nations. Economic and Social Council. Human rights questions. Capital punishment. Report of the Secretary-General 1980. (E/1980/9 and Corr. 1 and 2, Add. 1 and Corr. 1 and Add. 2 and 3).
United Nations. Economic and Social Council. Procedure for the study of the question of capital punishment. (E/RES/747), 6 April 1960. . In Economic and Social Council Official Records, 29th Session, 1960, Suppl. 1, p. 4.
United Nations. Economic and Social Council. Social development questions : capital punishment. Report of the Secretary-General, 26 April 1985, 48 p. (E/1985/43).
United Nations. Economic and Social Council. Safeguard guaranteeing protection of the rights of those facing the death penalty. (E/RES/1984/50). In Resolutions and decisions adopted by the Economic and Social Council at its 1st regular session of 1984, 5 June 1984, p. 73-74.
United Nations. Economic and Social Council. Social Commission. Capital punishment. In Report of the Ad Hoc Advisory Committee of Experts on the Prevention of Crime and the Treatment of Offenders, 1 February 1963, p. 14-34. (E/CN.5/371).
United Nations. General Assembly. Capital Punishment. In Crime prevention and control – Report of the Third Committee, 25 November 1977, p. 9-10 and 16-17. (A/32/359).
United Nations. Economic and Social Council. Capital punishment. (A/RES/1918/XVIII), 5 December 1963. In General Assembly Official Records, 18th Session, 1963, Suppl. 15, p. 40.
United Nations. Economic and Social Council. Capital punishment. (A/RES/2334/XXII), 18 December 1967. In General Assembly Official Records, 22nd Session, 1967, suppl. 16, p. 40.
United Nations. Economic and Social Council. Capital punishment. (A/RES/2393/XXIII), 26 November 1968. In General Assembly Official Records, 23rd Session, 1968, suppl. 18, p. 4.
United Nations. Economic and Social Council. Capital punishment in Southern Africa. (A/RES/2394/XXIII), 26 November 1968. In General Assembly Official Records, 23rd Session, 1968, suppl. 18, p. 42.
United Nations. Economic and Social Council. Capital punishment. (A/RES/2857/XXVI), 20 December 1971. In General Assembly Official Records, 26th Session, 1971, suppl. 29, p. 94.
United Nations. Economic and Social Council. Capital punishment. (A/RES/3011/XXVII), 18 December 1972. In General Assembly Official Records, 27th Session, 1972, suppl. 30, p. 67.

United Nations. Economic and Social Council. Capital punishment. (A/RES/32/61), 8 December 1977. In General Assembly Official Records, 32nd Session, 1977, suppl. 45, p. 136.
United Nations. Economic and Social Council. Capital punishment. (A/RES/35/437), 15 December 1980. In General Assembly Official Records, 35th Session, 1980/1981, suppl. 40, p. 288.
United Nations. Economic and Social Council. Capital punishment. Resolution 36/59, 25 November 1981. In General Assembly Official Records, 36th Session, 1981/1982, suppl. 51, p. 174.
United Nations. General Assembly. Capital punishment. In Report of the Economic and Social Council. Report of the Third Committee, 11 December 1972, p. 11 (A/8928).
United Nations. General Assembly. Capital punishment. In Report of the Economic and Social Council on the work of its 52nd and 53rd Sessions. General Assembly Official Records, 27th Session, 1972, suppl. 3, p. 59-60.
United Nations. General Assembly. Capital punishment. In Report of the Economic and Social Council on the work of its organizational session for 1975 and of its 58th and 59th Session. General Assembly Official Records, 30th Session, 1975, suppl. 3, p. 47-48.
United Nations. General Assembly. Capital punishment. Report of the Third Committee, 10 November 1968, 18 p. (A/7303).
United Nations. General Assembly. Elaboration of a 2nd optional protocol to the International Covenant on Civil and Political Rights, aiming at the abolition of the death penalty, 15 February 1985, 2 p. (A/RES/39/137).
United Nations. General Assembly. Human rights in the administration of justice : resolution, 4 February 1985, 3 p. (A/RES/39/118).
United Nations. General Assembly. International covenants on human rights. Capital punishment : resolution, 4 February 1983, 2 p. (A/RES/37/192).
United Nations. General Assembly. International convenants on human rights. Elaboration of a 2nd optional protocol to the International Covenant on Civil and Political Rights, aiming at the abolition of the death penalty : report of the Secretary-General, 30 September 1982, 12 p. (A/37/407) and 1 October 1982, 6 p. (A/37/407/Add. 1).
United Nations. General Assembly. Study of the question of capital punishment. (A/RES/1396). In General Assembly Official Records, 14th Session, 1959, suppl. 16, p. 23.
United Nations. General Assembly. Seventh United Nations Congress on the Prevention of Crime and the Treatment of Offenders. Report of the African Regional Preparatory Meeting, 1983, p. 14 (A/CONF.121/RPM/4).
United Nations. General Assembly. Seventh United Nations Congress on the Prevention of Crime and the Treatment of Offenders. Report of the Asia and Pacific Regional Preparatory Meeting, 1983, p. 22 (A/CONF.121/RPM/2).
United Nations. General Assembly. Seventh United Nations Congress on the Prevention of Crime and the Treatment of Offenders. Report of the

European Regional Preparatory Meeting, 1983, p. 26 (A/CONF.121/RPM/1).
United Nations. General Assembly. Seventh United Nations Congress on the Prevention of Crime and the Treatment of Offenders. Report of the Latin American Regional Preparatory Meeting, 1983, p. 20 (A/CONF.121/RPM/3).
United Nations. General Assembly. Seventh United Nations Congress on the Prevention of Crime and the Treatment of Offenders. Report of the Western Asia Regional Preparatory Meeting, 1984, p. 21 (A/CONF.121/RPM/5).
United Nations. General Assembly. Survey of redress, assistance, restitution and compensation for victims of crime : report of the Secretary-General (A/CONF.121.4).
United Nations. Secretariat. Capital punishment. Information from governments compiled by the United Nations Secretariat, 15 September 1972, 84 p. (ST/SOA/118).
United Nations Social Defence Research Institute (UNSDRI). Commentary and bibliography on capital punishment. Rome, UNSDRI, April 1971, 32 p.
United Nations Social Defence Research Institute (UNSDRI). International bibliography on capital punishment. Rome, UNSDRI, 1978, 94 p.
United Nations Social Defence Research Institute (UNSDRI). International bibliography on capital punishment, 1978-1984. Rome, 1984, 52 p.
United States. California. Constitutional issues relative to death penalty : special hearing of the Assembly Committee on Criminal Justice, 1977. Sacramento, CA, 1977, 61 p.
United States. California. Assembly Judiciary Committee. Subcommittee on Capital Punishment. Report... pertaining to the problems of the death penalty and its administration in California. Sacramento, CA, 18 January 1957, 55 p.
United States. California. Senate Judiciary Committee. Report and testimony... (on a proposed bill) to abolish the death penalty. Sacramento, CA, 1960, 176 p.
United States. Congress. House Committee of the Judiciary. Hearing... on H.R. 870 to abolish the death penalty. Washington, D.C., Government Printing Office, May 1960, 181 p.
United States. Congress. Senate. Committee on the Judiciary. Death penalty legislation. Hearing before the Senate Committe S. 239, September 24, 1985. Washington, D.C., GPO, 1986, 107 p.
United States. Congress. Senate. Committee on the Judiciary. To establish rational criteria for the imposition of capital punishment. Hearings before the Senate Committee, S 1382, 95th Congress, 2nd Session. April 27-May 11, 1978. Washington, DC., Government Printing Office, 1978, 424 p.
United States. Congress. Senate. Committee on the Judiciary. Subcommittee on Criminal Law. To establish constitutional procedures for the imposition of capital punishment. Hearing before the Senate Subcommittee, S 1382, May 18, 1977. Washington, D.C., Government Printing Office, 1977, 338 p.
United States. Department of Justice. Bureau of Justice Statistics. Capital

punishment. 1979. Washington, D.C., Government Printing Office, 1980, 121 p. (National Prisoner Statistics, NCJ 70945).
United States. Department of Justice. Bureau of Justice Statistics. Capital Punishment. 1980. Washington, D.C., Government Printing Office, 1981, 97 p. (National Prisoner Statistics. NCJ 78600).
United States. Department of Justice. Bureau of Justice Statistics. Capital Punishment. 1981. Washington, D.C., Government Printing Office, 1982, 100 p. (National Prisoner Statistics. NCJ 86484).
United States. Department of Justice. Bureau of Justice Statistics. Capital Punishment. 1982. Washington, D.C., Government Printing Office, 1984, 99 p. (National Prisoner Statistics. NCJ 91533).
United States. Department of Justice. Bureau of Justice Statistics. Capital Punishment. 1983. Washington, D.C., Government Printing Office, 1986, 95 p. (National Prisoner Statistics. NCJ 99561).
United States. Department of Justice. Bureau of Justice Statistics. Capital Punishment. 1984. Washington, D.C., Government Printing Office, 1986, 97 p. (National Prisoner Statistics. NCJ 99562).
United States. Department of Justice. Bureau of Prisons. Capital Punishment 1930-1968. Washington, D.C., Government Printing Office, 1969, 30 p. (National Prisoner Statistics, Bulletin no. 45).
United States. Department of Justice. Bureau of Prisons. Capital Punishment 1930-1970. Washington, D.C., Government Printing Office, 1971, 50 p. (National Prisoner Statistics, Bulletin no. 46).
United States. National Criminal Justice Information and Statistics Service. Capital Punishment 1971-1972. Washington, D.C., Government Printing Office, 1974, 59 p. (National Prisoner Statistics, Bulletin no. SD-NPS-CP-1).
United States. National Criminal Justice Information and Statistics Service. Capital Punishment 1973. Washington, D.C., Government Printing Office, 1975, 60 p. (National Prisoner Statistics, Bulletin no. SD-NPS-CP-2).
United States. National Criminal Justice Information and Statistics Service. Capital Punishment 1974. Washington, D.C., Government Printing Office, November 1975, 58 p. (National Prisoner Statistics, Bulletin no. SD-NPS-CP-3).
United States. National Criminal Justice Information and Statistics Service. Capital Punishment 1975. Washington, D.C., Government Printing Office, 1975, 56 p. (National Prisoner Statistics, no. SD-NPS-CP-4).
United States. National Criminal Justice Information and Statistics Service. Capital Punishment 1976. Washington, D.C., Government Printing Office, 1977, 61 p. (National Prisoner Statistics, Bulletin no. SD-NPS-CP-5).
United States. National Criminal Justice Information and Statistics Service. Capital Punishment 1977. Washington, D.C., Government Printing Office, 1978, 96 p. (National Prisoner Statistics, Bulletin no. SD-NPS-CP-6).
United States. National Criminal Justice Information and Statistics Ser-

vice. Capital Punishment 1978. Washington, D.C., Government Printing Office, 1979, 91 p. (National Prisoner Statistics, Bulletin no. SD-NPS-CP-7).

United States. Florida. Special Commission for the Study of Abolition of Death Penalty in Capital Cases. Report 1963-1965. Tallahassee, FL, 1965.

United States. Maryland. Legislative Council Committee. Report of the Legislative Council Committee on Capital Punishment. Baltimore, MD, 1962, 80 p.

United States. Massachusetts. Special Commission established for the Purpose of investigating and studying the abolition of the death penalty in capital cases. Report and recommendations. Boston, MA, 1958, 120 p. (House Document 2575).

United States. Michigan. State Bar Association. Committee on Capital Punishment. Report. Michigan State Bar Journal. Lansing, MI : 278-305, November 1928.

United States. New York. Commission on Capital Punishment. Report. Albany, N.Y., Argus Company, 1888, 100 p.

United States. New York. District Attorney's Association. Symposium on capital punishment. New York Law Forum. New York, N.Y. : 247-319, August 1961.

United States. New York. Temporary Commission on Revision of the Penal Law and Criminal Code. Special report on capital punishment. Albany, N.Y., March 1965.

United States. New York. Probation and Parole Officiers Association. Juvenile justice : a formula for the future. Probation and Parole. New York, N.Y., 7, 1975.

United States. North Carolina. Board of Charities and Public Welfare. Capital punishment in North Carolina. Raleigh, N.C., 1929, 173 p.

United States. Ohio. Legislative Service Commission. Capital punishment. Columbus, OH, January 1961, 88 p. (Staff Research Report no. 46).

United States. Pennsylvania. Governor's Study Commission on Capital Punishment. Report. Harrisburg, PA, 1973, 135 p.

United States. Pennsylvania. Joint Legislative Committee on Capital Punishment. Report. Harrisburg, PA, June 1961, 32 p.

United States. Wisconsin. Legislative Reference Library. Capital Punishment in the States with special reference to Wisconsin. Madison, WI, 1962, 12 p.

The University of Chicago. Center for Studies in Criminal Justice. A selected international bibliography on capital punishment. Chicago, IL, Center for Studies in Criminal Justice, 1968, 55 p.

University of South Florida. Department of Criminology. Liberty and justice for all ? : a question and answer pamphlet about the death penalty. Tempe, FL, University of South Florida, 1986, 118 p.

Upadhyaya, S.K. *Capital punishment in a changing society (special reference to India).* Indian Journal of Criminology and Criminalistics. New Delhi, 2/3 : 197-201, 1982, no. 4.

Urofsky, M.I. *A right to die : termination of appeal for condemned prisoners.* Journal of Criminal Law and Criminology. Chicago, IL, 75 : 553-582, 1984, no. 3.

Ursic, M. *Crni ritual smrtne kazni (The Black ritual of the death penalty).* Ljubljana, Delo, 1982.

Valderez Ayres Neves de Alencar, A. *Pena de morte (Capital punishment).* Revista de Informacao Legislative. Rio de Janeiro, 8 : 121-196, 1971, no. 29.

Valencia, G. *La pena de muerte : texto íntegro de su intervención en el Senado de la República de 1925 (Capital punishment : full text of his speech in the Senate in 1925).* Bogotá, Edición Publicitaria, 1974.

Vallenga, J.J. *Christianity and the death penalty. In* The death penalty in America ; an anthology. Edited by H.A. Bedau. Garden City, N.Y. Anchor Books, 1964, p. 123-130.

Van den Haag, E. *Comment on John Kaplan's « Administering capital punishment ».* University of Florida Law Review. Gainesville, FL, 36 : 193-199, 1984.

Van den Haag, E. and Conrad, J.P. *The death penalty : a debate.* New York, N.Y., Plenum, 1983, 320 p.

Van den Haag, E. *In defence of the death penalty : a legal-practical-moral analysis.* Criminal Law Bulletin. Boston, MA, 14 : 51-68, 1978, no. 1.

Van den Haag, E. *In defence of the death penalty : a practical and moral analysis. In* The death penalty in America. Edited by H.A. Bedau, 3rd ed. Oxford. Oxford University Press, 1982, p. 323-332.

Van den Haag, E. *On deterrence and the death penalty.* Journal of Criminal Law, Criminology and Police Science. Baltimore, MD, 60 : 141-147, June 1969.

Van den Haag, E. *Refuting Reiman and Nathason.* Philosophy and Public Affairs. Princeton, N.J., 14 : 165-176, 1985, no. 2.

Van den Haag, E. *The ultimate punishment : a defence.* Harvard Law Review. Cambridge, MA, 99 : 1662-1669, May 1986.

Van der Berg, G.P. *The Soviet Union and the death penalty.* Soviet Studies. Glasgow, 35 : 154-174, 1983, no. 2.

Van Niekerk, B. *Hanged by the neck until you are dead.* South African Law Journal. Cape Town, 86 : 457-475, November 1969.

Van Niekerk, B. *Hanged by the neck.* South African Law Journal. Cape Rown, 87 : 60-75, 1970.

Van Niekerk, B. *Popular attitudes on crime and justice.* South African Journal of Criminal Law and Criminology. Durban, 5 : 16-21, 1981, no. 1.

Vance, C.S. *The death penalty after Furman.* Prosecutor. Chicago, IL, 9 : 307-311, 1973, no. 4.

Vandiver, M. and Radelet, M.L. *Bibliography* (on the death penalty). Gainesville, FL, Department of Sociology, University of Florida, 1986, 36 p.

Vecilla de las Heras, L. *La iglesia y la pena capital (The church and capital punishment).* Revista de Estudios Penitenciarios. Madrid, 167 : 653-680, 1964.

Vené, G.F. *Pena di morte. Quelli di Villarbasse : gli ultimi giustiziati in Italia (Capital punishment. Those from Villarbasse : the last ones executed in Italy).* Milano, Bompiani, 1984, 250 p.

Vernet, J. *La chiesa e la pena di morte (The church and the death penalty).* Scuola Positiva. Milano : 620-625, 1962.
Vernet, J. *Condamnés pour toujours ? (Sentenced for ever ?)* Revue de Science Criminelle et de Droit Pénal Comparé. Paris : 517-524, 1960.
Vernet, J. *Directives et prospectives de l'église sur la peine de mort (Directives and perspectives of the church on the death penalty).* Revue de Science Criminelle et de Droit Pénal Comparé. Paris : 201-204, janvier-mars 1970.
Vernet, J. *Enquête préalable à l'abolition de la peine de mort : la perpétuité de la peine de remplacement est-elle funeste ? (Enquiry prior to the abolition of the death penalty : is the substitutive life sentence obnoxious ?)* Revue de Science Criminelle et de Droit Pénal Comparée. Paris : 579-597, 1966.
Vernet, J. *Enquête sur la détention de longue durée dans les pays d'Europe qui ont aboli la peine de mort (Survey on long term detention in the European countries which have abolished capital punishment).* Annales de Médecine Légale. Paris : 356-360, 1966.
Vernet, J. *La glaive et la croix : position de l'église devant la peine de mort (The blade and the cross : the church's position regarding capital punishment).* Revue Internationale de Criminologie et de Police Technique. Genève, 4 : 63-65, janvier-mars 1955.
Vernet, J. *Peine capitale, peine perdue (Capital punishment, lost punishment).* Etudes. Paris : 193-209, Novembre 1962.
Viader Vives, A. *Historia del castigo (The history of punishment).* Barcelona, ed. Antalbe, 1974, 458 p.
Viaud, J. *La peine de mort en matière politique (The death penalty regarding political matters).* Paris, Arthur Rousseau, 1902.
Vidmar, N. and Dittenhoffer, T. *Informed public opinion and death penalty attitudes.* Canadian Journal of Criminology. Ottawa, Ont., 23 : 43-56, 1981, no. 1.
Vidmar, N. and Ellsworth P.C. *Public opinion on the death penalty.* Stanford Law Review. Stanford, CA, 26 : 1245-1270, June 1974. Also in Capital punishment un the United States. Edited by H.A. Bedau and C.M. Pierce. New York, N.Y., AMS Press, 1976, p. 125-151.
Vidmar, N. *Retributive and utilitarian motives and other correlates of Canadian attitudes toward the death penalty.* Canadian Psychologist. Montreal, Ont., 15 : 337-356, 1974, no. 4.
Vidmar, N. and Miller, D. *Socio-psychological processes underlying attitudes toward legal punishment.* Law and Society Review. Denver, CO, 14 : 565-603, 1980, no. 3.
Viennet, G. *Association française contre la peine de mort (The French Association against the Death Penalty).* Revue de Droit Pénal et de Criminologie. Bruxelles, 59 : 23-24, 1979, no. 1.
Villegas, A.C. *Le pena de muerte (Capital punishment).* Bogotà, A.C., Villegas, 1965.
Vocca, O. *Evoluzione del pensiero criminologico sulla pena di morte : da Cesare Beccaria al Codice Zanardelli (The evolution of criminological thought on capital punishment : from Cesare Beccaria to the Zanardelli Code).* Napoli, Jovene, 1984, 301 p.
Vold, G. *Extent and trend of capital crimes in the United States.* Annals

of the American Academy of Political and Social Science. Philadelphia, PA, no. 284 : 1-7, 1952.
Vold, G. *Can the death penalty prevent crime ?* Prison Journal. Philadelphia, PA : 3-8, October 1932.
Vouin, R. *L'article de la mort (The articles of death).* Revue de Science Criminelle et de Droit Pénal Comparé. Paris : 559-577, 1966.
Waldo, G.P. *The death penalty and deterrence : a review of recent research. In* The mad, the bad and the different. Lexington, MA, Lexington Books, 1982, p. 169-178.
Waldo, G.P. and Chiricos, T. *Perceived penal sanction and self-reported criminality : a neglected approach to deterrence research.* Social Problems. South Bend, IN, 19 : 522, 1972.
Walker, N. *Crimes, courts and figures.* Baltimore, MD, Penguin Books Inc., 1971.
Ward, B. *Competency for executions : problems in law and psychiatry.* Florida State University Law Review. Tallahassee, FL, 14 : 35-107, 1986.
Warr, M. and Stafford, M. *Public goals of punishment and support for the death penalty.* Journal of Research in Crime and Delinquency. Beverly Hills, CA, 21 : 95-112, 1984, no. 2.
Washington Research Project. The case against capital punishment. Washington, D.C., 1971, 68 p.
Wasserman, I.A. *Non-deterrent effect of executions on homicide rates.* Psychological Reports. Missoula, MT, 48 : 137-138, 1981, no. 1.
Wechsler, H. *The definition of specific crimes : problems of coverage and grading. In* Crime, criminology and public policy. Edited by T. Hood. London, Heinemann Educational Books Ltd., 1974, p. 450-454.
Weihofen, H. *The urge to punish : new approaches to the problem of mental irresponsibility for crime.* New York, N.Y., Farrar, Straus, and Cudahy, 1956, 213 p.
Weiland, S.C. and Jones, G. *Federal procedural implications of Furman v. Georgia : what rights for the formerly capital offender ?* American Journal of Criminal Law. Austin, TX, 1 : 107-147, October 1972.
Weisberg, R. *Deregulating death.* Supreme Court Review : 305-395, 1983.
Wellek, J.A. *Eighth amendment-trial court may impose death sentence despite jury's recommendation of life imprisonment.* Spaziano v. Florida 104 S. Ct. 3154 (1984). Journal of Criminal Law and Criminology. Chicago, IL, 75 : 813-838, 1984, no. 3.
Welling, B. and Hipfner, L.A. *Cruel and unusual ? : capital punishment in Canada.* University of Toronto Law Journal. Toronto, Ont., 26 : 58-83, Winter 1976.
Wells, C. *The death penalty for provocation ?* Criminal Law Review. London : 662-672, November 1978.
Welsh, D. *Capital punishment in South Africa. In* African penal systems. Edited by A. Milner. London, Routledge and Kegan Paul, 1969, p. 397-427.
Werkheiser, R.M. and Barnhart, A.C. *Capital punishment.* New York, N.Y., The National Council of the Episcopal Church, 1961, 32 p.
West, E.S. *The right of confrontation and reliability in capital sentencing.* Proffitt v. Wainright 685 F.2nd 1227 (11th Cir. 1982). American Criminal Law Review. Washington, D.C., 20 : 599-615, 1983, no. 4.

West, L.L. *Psychiatric reflections on the death penalty.* American Journal of Orthopsychiatry. Albany, N.Y., 45 : 689-700, 1975, no. 4 Also in Capital punishment in the United States. Edited by H.A. Bedau and C.M. Pierce. New York, N.Y. AMS Press, 1976, p. 419-431.

Wexley, J. *The judgment of Julius and Ethel Rosenberg.* New York, N.Y., Cameron and Klahn, 1955, 672 p.

Weyl, S.E. *The supreme judicial court and the death penalty : the effects of judicial choice on legislative opinion.* Boston University Law Review. Boston, MA, 54 : 158-185, 1974, no. 1.

Wheeler, J. *The death penalty.* Police Review. London, 90 : 734, 1982, no. 4653.

Wheeler, M. *Toward a theory of limited punishment : an examination of the eighth amendment.* Stanford Law Review. Stanford, CA, 24 : 836-873, May 1972.

White, B. *The murderers of Gloucestershire : hangings in Gloucester prison (and others), 1827-1939.* Gloucester, Bryan White, 1985, 65 p.

White, D.D. *To die is not enough : a true account of murder and retribution.* Boston, MA, Houghton Mifflin Company, 1974, 238 p.

White, W.S. *The constitutional invalidity of convictions imposed by death-qualified juries.* Cornell University Law Review. Ithaca, N.Y., 58 : 1176-1220, July 1971.

White, W.S. *Life in the balance : procedural safeguards in capital cases.* Ann. Arbor, MI, University of Michigan Press, 1984, 289 p.

White, W.S. *The psychiatric examination and the fifth amendment privilege in capital cases.* Journal of Criminal Law and Criminology. Chicago, IL, 74 : 943-990, 1983, no. 3.

White, W.S. *The role of the social sciences in determining the constitutionality of capital punishment.* American Journal of Orthopsychiatry. Albany, N.Y., 45 : 581-595, 1975, no. 4, Also in Capital punishment in the United States. Edited by H.A. Bedau and C. Pierce, New York, N.Y., AMS Press, 1976, p. 3-23.

White, W.S. *Waiver and the death penalty : the implications of Estelle v. Smith.* Journal of Criminal Law and Criminology. Chicago, IL, 72 : 1522-1549, 1981, no. 4.

Who's qualified to decide who dies ? Nebraska Law Review. Lincoln, NE, 65 : 558-583, 1986.

Williams, E.B. *Capital punishment.* Trial. Washington, D.C., 1 : 39-42, April-May 1965.

Williams, F. *The death penalty and the negro.* Crisis, New York, N.Y., 67 : 501-512, 1960.

Wilson, W. *Juvenile offenders and the electric chair : cruel and unusual punishment or firm discipline for the hopelessly delinquent ?* University of Florida Law Review. Gainesville, FL, 35 : 344-371, 1983, no. 2.

Wingersky, M.F. *Report of the Royal Commission on Capital Punishment.* Journal of Criminal Law. Bishop's Stortford, U.K. : 695-716, March-April 1954.

Winick, B. *Prosecutorial peremptory challenge practices in capital cases : an empirical study and constitutional analysis.* Michigan Law Review. Ann Arbor, MI, 81 : 1-98, 1982.

Winick, B. *Witherspoon in Florida : reflections on the challenge for cause of juniors in capital cases in a State in which the judge makes the sentencing decision.* University of Miami Law Review. Miami, FL, 37 : 82-866, 1983.
Witherspoon, B. *Death row.* New York, N.Y., Pyramid Publications Inc., 1968, 189 p.
Wolf, E. *Abstracts of analysis of jury sentencing in capital cases : New Jersey, 1937-64.* Rutgers Law Review. Newark, N.J., 19 : 56-64, 1965.
Wolfe, B.H. *Pileup on death row.* New York, N.Y., Doubleday and Company Inc., 1973, 439 p.
Wolfgang, M.E., Kelly, A. and Nolde, H. *Comparison of the executed and commuted among admissions to death row.* Journal of Criminal Law, Criminology and Police Science. Baltimore, MD, 53 : 301-311, 1962.
Wolfgang, M.E. *The death penalty : social philosophy and social science research.* Criminal Law Bulletin. Boston, MA, 14 : 18-33, 1978, no. 1.
Wolfgang, M.E., Kelly, A. and Nolde, H.C. *Executions and commutations in Pennsylvania. In* The death penalty in America ; an anthology. Edited by H.A. Bedau. Garden City, N.Y., Anchor Books, 1964, p. 464-488.
Wolfgang, M.E. *Murder, the pardon board, and recommendations by judges and district attorneys.* Journal of Criminal Law, Criminology and Police Science. Baltimore, MD, 50 : 338-346, November-December 1959.
Wolfgang, M.E. *Patterns in criminal homicide.* Philadelphia, PA, University of Pennsylvania Press, 1958.
Wolfgang, M.E. and Riedel, M. *Race, discretion and the death penalty : final report.* Center of Studies in Criminology and Criminal Law, University of Pennsylvania, March 1979, 197 p.
Wolfgang, M.E. and Riedel, M. *Race, judicial discretion, and the death penalty.* Annals of the American Academy of Political and Social Science. Philadelphia, PA, 407 : 119-133, May 1973.
Wolfgang, M.E. *Racial discrimination in the death sentence for rape. In* Executions in America. Edited by W. Bowers, Lexington, MA, Lexington Books, 1974.
Wolfgang, M.E. and Riedel, M. *Racial discrimination, rape and the death penalty. In* The death penalty in America. Edited by H.A. Bedau, 3rd ed. Oxford University Press, 1982, p. 194-205.
Wolfgang, M.E. and Riedel, M. *Rape, race and the death penalty in Georgia.* American Journal of Orthopsychiatry. Albany, N.Y., 45 : 658-668, 1975, no. 4.
Wolfgang, M.E. and Riedel, M. *Rape, race discrimination, and the death penalty. In* Capital punishment in the United States. Edited by H.A. Bedau and C.M. Pierce, New York, N.Y., AMS Press, 1976, p. 99-123.
Wolfgang, M.E. *A sociological analysis of criminal homicide. In* The death penalty in America ; an anthology. Edited by H.A. Bedau. Garden City, N.Y., Anchor Books, 1964, p. 74-89.
Wolfson, W.P. *The deterrent effect of the death penalty upon prison murder. In* The death penalty in America. Edited by H.A. Bedau. 3rd ed. Oxford University Press, 1982, p. 159-172.
Wolpin, K.I. *Capital punishment and homicide in England : a summary*

of results. American Economic Review. Nashville, TN, 68 : 422-427, 1978, no. 2.

Wood, A.L. *The alternatives to the death penalty.* Annals of the American Academy of Political and Social Science. Philadelphia, PA, 284 : 63-72, November 1952.

Wootton, B. *Morality and mistakes. In* The hanging question. Edited by L. Blom-Cooper. London, Duckworth and Co., 1969, 138 p.

Yagimoto, M. *(Abolition of capital punishment in Great Britain).* Horitsu Jiho. Japan, 42 : 27, May 1970, In Japanese.

Yanez Roman, P. *Anticonstitucionalidad de la pena de muerte en los Estados Unidos de América. Parte I (The anticonstitutionality of capital punishment in the United States, Part I).* Anuario de Derecho Penal y Ciencias Penales. Madrid, 26 : 231-296, mayo-agosto 1973.

Yanez Roman, P. *Anticonstitucionalidad de la pena de muerte en los Estados Unidos de América. Parte II (The anticonstitutionality of capital punishment in the United States, Part II).* Anuario de Derecho Penal y Ciencias Penales. Madrid, 27 : 265-328, mayo-agosto 1974.

Yetter, J.F. *Florida's death penalty – is it unconstitutional under State law ?* Florida Bar Journal. Tallahassee, FL, 52 : 372, May 1978.

Yetter, J.F. *Gardner v. Florida : pre-sentence reports in capital sentencing procedures.* Ohio Northern University Law Review. Ada, OH, 5 : 175, 1978.

Yoder, J.H. *The christian and capital punishment.* Newton, KS, Faith and Life Press, 1961.

Yoder, J.H. *A christian perspective. In* The death penalty in America. Edited by H.A. Bedau, 3rd ed. Oxford. Oxford University Press, 1982, p. 370-374.

Younger, K. *The historical perspective. In* The hanging question. Edited by L. Blom-Cooper. London, Duckworth and Co., 1969, p. 5-12.

Yunker, J.A. *Is the death penalty a deterrent to homicide ? Some time series evidence.* Journal of Behavioral Economics. Macomb, IL, 6 : 361-397, 1977, no. 1-2.

Yunker, J.A. *Old controversy renewed : introduction to the Journal of Behavioral Economics capital punishment symposium.* Journal of Behavioral Economics. Macomb, IL, 6 : 1-32, 1977, no. 1-2.

Yunker, J.A. *The relevance of the identification problem to statistical research on capital punishment : a comment on McGahey.* Crime and Delinquency. Hackensack, N.J., 28 : 96-124, 1982, no. 1.

Yunker, J.A. *Testing the deterrent effect of capital punishment.* Criminology. Gainesville, FL, 19 : 626-649, 1982, no. 4.

Zajadlo, J. *Zniesienie káry śmierci w zachodnioruropejskim systemia miedzynarodowej ochrony praw czlowieka (The abolition of capital punishment within the Western European system of the international protection of human rights).* Palestra, Warsaw, no. 5-6, 1984.

Zeisel, H. *A comment on " the deterrent effect of capital punishment " by Phillips.* American Journal of Sociology. Chicago, IL, 88 : 167-169, 1982, no. 1.

Zeisel, H. *The deterrent effect of the death penalty : facts v. faith. In* The supreme court review, 1975. Edited by P. Kurland. Chicago, University of Chicago Press, 1977, p. 317-343.

Zeisel, H. *Race bias in the administration of the death penalty : the Florida experience.* Harvard Law Review. Cambridge, MA, 95 : 456-468, 1981, no. 2.
Zeisel, H. *Some data on juror attitudes towards capital punishment.* Chicago, IL, Center for Studies in Criminal Justice, University of Chicago, 1968, 52 p.
Zelikow, P.D. *Constitutionality of imposing the death penalty for felony murder.* Houston Law Review. Houston, TX, 15 : 356-386, 1978.
Zelmanowits, J. *Is there such a thing as capital punishment ?* British Journal of Criminology. London, 2 : 78-80, July 1961.
Zimmerman, I. *Punishment without crime.* New York, N.Y. Potter Inc., 1963, 304 p.
Zimring, F.E. and Hawkins G.J. *Capital punishment and the American agenda.* New York, N.Y. Cambridge University Press, 1986.
Zimring, F.E. and Hawkins G.J. *Capital punishment and the eighth amendment : Furman and Greg in retrospect.* University of California Davis Law Review. Davis, CA, 18 : 927-956, 1985.
Zimring, F.E. and Hawkins G.J. *Deterrence : the legal threat in crime control.* Chicago, IL, University of Chicago Press, 1973, 376 p.
Zimring, F.E., Eigen, J. and O'Malley, S. *The going price of criminal homicide in Philadelphia. In* Capital punishment in the United States. Edited by H.A. Bedau and C.M. Pierce. New York, N.Y., AMS Press, 1976, p. 76-98.
Zimring, F.E., Eigen, J and O'Malley, S. *Punishing homicide in Philadelphia : perspectives on the death penalty.* University of Chicago Law Review. Chicago, IL, 43 : 227-252, Winter 1976.
Zinna, F.J. and Cavanagh, T.W. Jr. *The constitutionality and desirability of bifurcated trials and sentencing standards.* Seton Hall Law Review. Newark, N.J., 2 : 427-442, 1971, no. 2.
Zvekic, U., Saito, F. and Ghirlando, N. *Main trends in research on capital punishment, 1979-1983.* Crime Prevention and Criminal Justice Newsletter. Vienna, no. 12/13 : 54-61, November 1986. Also in Japanese : Japanese Journal of Criminal Psychology. Tokyo, 23 : 59-73, 1985, no. 1. Also in French : Revue Internationale de Criminologie et de Police Technique. Genève, 39 : 328-338, 1986, no. 3.

LIST OF UNSDRI PUBLICATIONS AND STAFF PAPERS

1969 Publ. No. 1 TENDENCIAS Y NECESIDADES DE LA INVESTIGACION CRIMINOLOGICA EN AMERICA LATINA [1]. *F. Ferracuti, R. Bergalli.*

1970 Publ. No. 2 MANPOWER AND TRAINING IN THE FIELD OF SOCIAL DEFENCE [2]. *F. Ferracuti, M.C. Giannini.*

1971 S.P. No. 1 CO-ORDINATION OF INTERDISCIPLINARY RESEARCH IN CRIMINOLOGY [1]. *F. Ferracuti.*

1971 Publ. No. 3 SOCIAL DEFENCE IN UGANDA: A SURVEY OF RESEARCH [1].

1971 Publ. No. 4 PUBLIC ET JUSTICE: UNE ÉTUDE PILOTE EN TUNISIE [1]. *A. Bouhdiba.*

1972 S.P. No. 2 THE EVALUATION AND IMPROVEMENT OF MANPOWER TRAINING PROGRAMMES IN SOCIAL DEFENCE [1]. *R.W. Burnham.*

1972 S.P. No. 3 PERCEPTIONS OF DEVIANCE. SUGGESTIONS FOR CROSS-CULTURAL RESEARCH [1]. *G. Newman.*

1973 S.P. No. 4 PERCEPTION CLINIQUE ET PSYCHOLOGIQUE DE LA DÉVIANCE. *F. Ferracuti, G. Newman.*

SEXUAL DEVIANCE. A SOCIOLOGICAL ANALYSIS. *G. Newman.*

ASPETTI SOCIALI DEI COMPORTAMENTI DEVIANTI SESSUALI [1]. *F. Ferracuti, R. Lazzari.*

---

[1] Out of print.

[2] Also published in French and Spanish.

1973 S.P. No. 5 PSYCHOACTIVE DRUG CONTROL. ISSUES AND RECOMMENDATIONS[2]. *J.J. Moore, C.R.B. Joyce, J. Woodcock.*

1973 Publ. No. 5 MIGRATION. Report of the Research Conference on Migration, Ethnic Minority Status and Social Adaptation, Rome, 13-16 June 1972.

1973 Publ. No. 6 A PROGRAMME FOR DRUG USE RESEARCH. Report of the proceedings of a workshop at Frascati, Italy, 11-15 December 1972[1].

1973 S.P. No. 6 UN PROGRAMMA DI RICERCA SULLA DROGA. Rapporto del seminario di Frascati, 11-15 dicembre 1972[1].

1974 Publ. No. 7 A WORLD DIRECTORY OF CRIMINOLOGICAL INSTITUTES[1]. *B. Kasme* (ed.).

1974 Publ. No. 8 RECENT CONTRIBUTIONS TO SOVIET CRIMINOLOGY[1].

1974 Publ. No. 9 ECONOMIC CRISIS AND CRIME. Interim report and materials[1].

1974 Publ. No. 10 CRIMINOLOGICAL RESEARCH AND DECISION-MAKING. Studies on the influence of criminological research on criminal policy in The Netherlands and Finland[1].

1976 Publ. No. 11 EVALUATION RESEARCH IN CRIMINAL JUSTICE. Material and proceedings of a Research Conference convened in the context of the Fifth United Nations Congress on the Prevention of Crime and the Treatment of Offenders.

1976 Publ. No. 12 JUVENILE JUSTICE. An international survey, country reports, related materials and suggestions for future research[1].

---

[1] Out of print.

[2] Also published in French and Spanish.

1976 Publ. No. 13 THE PROTECTION OF THE ARTISTIC AND ARCHAEOLOGICAL HERITAGE. A VIEW FROM ITALY AND INDIA.

1976 Publ. No. 14 PRISON ARCHITECTURE. An international survey of representative closed institutions and analysis of current trends in prison design[3].

1976 Publ. No. 15 ECONOMIC CRISIS AND CRIME. Correlations between the state of the economy, deviance and the control of deviance[1].

1976 Publ. No. 16 INVESTIGATING DRUG ABUSE. A multinational programme of pilot studies into the non-medical use of drugs. *J.J. Moore.*

1978 Publ. No. 17 A WORLD DIRECTORY OF CRIMINOLOGICAL INSTITUTES (2nd edition)[1].

1978 Publ. No. 18 DELAY IN THE ADMINISTRATION OF CRIMINAL JUSTICE - INDIA. *S.K. Mukherjee, A. Gupta.*

1979 Publ. No. 19 RESEARCH AND DRUG POLICY. *J.J. Moore, L. Bozzetti.*

1981 THE EFFECT OF ISLAMIC LEGISLATION ON CRIME PREVENTION IN SAUDI ARABIA[4].

1982 Publ. No. 20 A WORLD DIRECTORY OF CRIMINOLOGICAL INSTITUTES (3rd edition)[1].

1984 Publ. No. 21 COMBATTING DRUG ABUSE. *F. Bruno.*

1984 Publ. No. 22 JUVENILE SOCIAL MALADJUSTMENT AND HUMAN RIGHTS IN THE CONTEXT OF URBAN DEVELOPMENT.

1984 Publ. No. 23 THE PHENOMENOLOGY OF KIDNAPPINGS IN SARDINIA. *I.F. Caramazza, U. Leone.*

---

[1] Out of print.

[3] Available through The Architectural Press, 9 Queen Anne's Gate, London SW-H 9BY.

[4] At the request of the Government of the Kingdom of Saudi Arabia, UNSDRI published English, French and Spanish editions of this publication.

1984 Publ. No. 24 THE ROLE OF THE JUDGE IN CONTEMPORARY SOCIETY[5].

1985 Publ. No. 25 CRIME AND CRIMINAL POLICY. PAPERS IN HONOUR OF MANUEL LOPEZ-REY. *P. David* (ed.).

1985 Publ. No. 26 FIRST JOINT INTERNATIONAL CONFERENCE ON RESEARCH IN CRIME PREVENTION, Riyad, 23-25 January 1984[6].

1986 Publ. No. 27 ACTION-ORIENTED RESEARCH ON YOUTH CRIME: AN INTERNATIONAL PERSPECTIVE. *U. Zvekić* (ed.).

1986 Publ. No. 28 A WORLD DIRECTORY OF CRIMINOLOGICAL INSTITUTES (4th Edition). *C. Masotti Santoro* (ed.).

1987 Publ. No. 29 RESEARCH AND INTERNATIONAL CO-OPERATION IN CRIMINAL JUSTICE: Survey on Needs and Priorities of Developing Countries. *U. Zvekić, A. Mattei.*

1988 Publ. No. 30 DRUGS AND PUNISHMENT: *D. Cotič.*

1988 Publ. No. 31 ANALYSING (IN)FORMAL MECHANISMS OF CRIME CONTROL: A Cross-cultural Perspective. *M. Findlay, U. Zvekić.*

1988 PRISON IN AFRICA: Acts of the Seminar for Heads of Penitentiary Administrations of the African Countries[7].

---

[1] Out of print.

[5] In collaboration with the International Association of Judges.

[6] In collaboration with the Arab Security Studies and Training Center.

[7] In collaboration with the Ministry of Justice of Italy and the International Centre for Sociological, Penal and Penitentiary Studies, Messina, Italy.

كيفية الحصول على منشورات الأمم المتحدة

يمكن الحصول على منشورات الأمم المتحدة من المكتبات ودور التوزيع في جميع أنحاء العالم . استعلم عنها من المكتبة التي تتعامل معها أو اكتب إلى : الأمم المتحدة ، قسم البيع في نيويورك أو في جنيف

如何购取联合国出版物

联合国出版物在全世界各地的书店和经售处均有发售。请向书店询问或写信到纽约或日内瓦的联合国销售组。

HOW TO OBTAIN UNITED NATIONS PUBLICATIONS

United Nations publications may be obtained from bookstores and distributors throughout the world. Consult your bookstore or write to: United Nations, Sales Section, New York or Geneva.

COMMENT SE PROCURER LES PUBLICATIONS DES NATIONS UNIES

Les publications des Nations Unies sont en vente dans les librairies et les agences dépositaires du monde entier. Informez-vous auprès de votre libraire ou adressez-vous à : Nations Unies, Section des ventes, New York ou Genève.

КАК ПОЛУЧИТЬ ИЗДАНИЯ ОРГАНИЗАЦИИ ОБЪЕДИНЕННЫХ НАЦИЙ

Издания Организации Объединенных Наций можно купить в книжных магазинах и агентствах во всех районах мира. Наводите справки об изданиях в вашем книжном магазине или пишите по адресу: Организация Объединенных Наций, Секция по продаже изданий, Нью-Йорк или Женева.

COMO CONSEGUIR PUBLICACIONES DE LAS NACIONES UNIDAS

Las publicaciones de las Naciones Unidas están en venta en librerías y casas distribuidoras en todas partes del mundo. Consulte a su librero o diríjase a: Naciones Unidas, Sección de Ventas, Nueva York o Ginebra.

inted in Rome
pografia Poliglotta della
ntificia Università Gregoriana,
a. della Pilotta, 4 - Roma
ly 1988
BN 92-9078-006-1

Price: .$US.25,00
(or equivalent in other
currencies)

United Nations publication
Sales No. E.88.III.N.3.